Hilda Hidalgo, PhD
Editor

Lesbians of Color:
Social and Human Services

Pre-publication
REVIEWS,
COMMENTARIES,
EVALUATIONS . . .

More pre-publication
REVIEWS, COMMENTARIES, EVALUATIONS . . .

". . . Offers a superior selection of voices that articulate the intensity and depth of lesbian consciousness. . . . The reader is provided with a racial and cultural kaleidoscope, as well as a cross section of social issues critical to lesbians of color. . . . challenges lesbians to utilize their unique "standpoint" to change white patriarchal and matriarchal constructs of society and to help 'remove institutional barriers which render people fearful, silent and disempowered, and which prevent both clients and service-providers from reaching full productivity and self-realization.'

Religious leaders will find insights about God's manifestation in the spirituality of lesbians. Human services administrators will benefit from the strategies in the book that provide new opportunities for lesbian professionals to participate fully in the creation of a just and liberating society.

. . . an excellent guide to organizational management and organizing efforts."

Rev. Alfonso A. Román, UCC
Special Assistant to the President, Bloomfield College

". . . Provides an insightful tool for mental health practitioners in the continuing effort to promote socio-cultural change. But it does more than that! It provides invaluable wisdom for those in positions which directly affect the growth of children–teachers. It speaks about layers of competence in working with lesbians of color–awareness, knowledge, and skills. It provides vehicles or prisms through which we can understand the patterns of discrimination which exist.

Dr. Hidalgo states that this book will "add some decibels of sound for a community whose voice has been so feeble in our social service literature." Schools and their inhabitants are an often overlooked subset of the social service community. As such, this book adds decibels of sound and is invaluable for teachers and other school personnel."

Elena J. Scambio, PhD
Former Superintendent of Schools, and Assistant Commissioner of Education, NJ
Family Therapist and Educational Consultant in NJ

Lesbians of Color:
Social and Human Services

Lesbians of Color: Social and Human Services

Hilda Hidalgo, PhD, ACSW
Editor

Lesbians of Color: Social and Human Services, edited by Hilda Hidalgo, was simultaneously issued by The Haworth Press, Inc., under the same title, as a special issue of *Journal of Gay & Lesbian Social Services*, Volume 3, Number 2 1995, James J. Kelly, Editor.

Harrington Park Press
An Imprint of
The Haworth Press, Inc.
New York • London

1-56023-072-X

Published by

Harrington Park Press, 10 Alice Street, Binghamton, NY 13904-1580 USA

Harrington Park Press is an imprint of The Haworth Press, Inc., 10 Alice Street, Binghamton, NY 13904-1580 USA.

Lesbians of Color: Social and Human Services has also been published as *Journal of Gay & Lesbian Social Services,* Volume 3, Number 2 1995.

The development, preparation, and publication of this work has been undertaken with great care. However, the publisher, employees, editors, and agents of The Haworth Press and all imprints of The Haworth Press, Inc., including The Haworth Medical Press and Pharmaceutical Products Press, are not responsible for any errors contained herein or for consequences that may ensue from use of materials or information contained in this work. Opinions expressed by the author(s) are not necessarily those of The Haworth Press, Inc.

Library of Congress Cataloging-in-Publication Data

Lesbians of color: social and human services / Hilda Hidalgo, editor.
    p. cm.
Includes bibliographical references and index.
ISBN 1-56024-751-7 (thp: alk. paper). – ISBN 1-56023-072-X (hpp: alk. paper)
1. Social work with lesbians--United States. 2. Social work with minorities--United States. 3. Lesbians--Services for--United States. 4. Minorities--Services for--United States. I. Hidalgo, Hilda.

HV1449.L494 1995   95-36538
362.83'08'693–dc20   CIP

Dedication

To Joan L. McEniry, because for thirty-five years you have been my loving life companion, and our relationship has helped me to be a better person.

H. H. (1995)

INDEXING & ABSTRACTING

Contributions to this publication are selectively indexed or abstracted in print, electronic, online, or CD-ROM version(s) of the reference tools and information services listed below. This list is current as of the copyright date of this publication. See the end of this section for additional notes.

- *AIDS Newsletter c/o CAB International/CAB ACCESS . . . available in print, diskettes updated weekly, and on INTERNET. Providing full bibliographic listings, author affiliation, augmented keyword searching,* CAB International, Wallingford Oxon OX10 8DE, United Kingdom

- *Cambridge Scientific Abstracts, Risk Abstracts,* Cambridge Information Group, 7200 Wisconsin Avenue #601, Bethesda, MD 20814

- *caredata CD: the social and community care database,* National Institute for Social Work, 5 Tavistock Place, London WC1H 9SS, England

- *Digest of Neurology and Psychiatry,* The Institute of Living, 400 Washington Street, Hartford, CT 06106

- *ERIC Clearinghouse on Urban Education (ERIC/CUE),* Teachers College, Columbia University, Box 40, New York, NY 10027

- *Family Life Educator "Abstracts Section,"* ETR Associates, P.O. Box 1830, Santa Cruz, CA 95061-1830

- *Homodok,* ILGA Archive, O.Z. Achterburgwal 185, NL-1012, DK Amsterdam, The Netherlands

- *Index to Periodical Articles Related to Law,* University of Texas, 727 East 26th Street, Austin, TX 78705

(continued)

- *INTERNET ACCESS (& additional networks) Bulletin Board for Libraries ("BUBL"), coverage of information resources on INTERNET, JANET, and other networks.*
  - JANET X.29: UK.AC.BATH.BUBL or 00006012101300
  - TELNET: BUBL.BATH.AC.UK or 138.38.32.45
    login 'bubl'
  - Gopher: BUBL.BATH.AC.UK (138.32.32.45). Port 7070
  - World Wide Web: http://www.bubl.bath.ac.uk./BUBL/ home.html
  - NISSWAIS telnetniss.ac.uk (for the NISS gateway)
  The Andersonian Library, Curran Building, 101 St. James Road, Glasgow G4 ONS, Scotland

- *Inventory of Marriage and Family Literature (online and hard copy),* National Council on Family Relations, 3989 Central Avenue NE, Suite 550, Minneapolis, MN 55421

- *Mental Health Abstracts (online through DIALOG),* IFI/Plenum Data Company, 3202 Kirkwood Highway, Wilmington, DE 19808

- *Referativnyi Zhurnal (Abstracts Journal of the Institute of Scientific Information of the Republic of Russia),* The Institute of Scientific Information, Baltijskaja ul., 14, Moscow A-219, Republic of Russia

- *Social Work Abstracts,* National Association of Social Workers, 750 First Street NW, 8th Floor, Washington, DC 20002

- *Sociological Abstracts (SA),* Sociological Abstracts, Inc., P.O. Box 22206, San Diego, CA 92192-0206

- *Studies on Women Abstracts,* Carfax Publishing Company, P.O. Box 25, Abingdon, Oxfordshire OX14 3UE, United Kingdom

- *Violence and Abuse Abstracts: A Review of Current Literature on Interpersonal Violence (VAA),* Sage Publications, Inc., 2455 Teller Road, Newbury Park, CA 91320

(continued)

SPECIAL BIBLIOGRAPHIC NOTES

related to special journal issues (separates)
and indexing/abstracting

☐ indexing/abstracting services in this list will also cover material in any "separate" that is co-published simultaneously with Haworth's special thematic journal issue or DocuSerial. Indexing/abstracting usually covers material at the article/chapter level.

☐ monographic co-editions are intended for either non-subscribers or libraries which intend to purchase a second copy for their circulating collections.

☐ monographic co-editions are reported to all jobbers/wholesalers/approval plans. The source journal is listed as the "series" to assist the prevention of duplicate purchasing in the same manner utilized for books-in-series.

☐ to facilitate user/access services all indexing/abstracting services are encouraged to utilize the co-indexing entry note indicated at the bottom of the first page of each article/chapter/contribution.

☐ this is intended to assist a library user of any reference tool (whether print, electronic, online, or CD-ROM) to locate the monographic version if the library has purchased this version but not a subscription to the source journal.

☐ individual articles/chapters in any Haworth publication are also available through the Haworth Document Delivery Services (HDDS).

CONTENTS

Foreword   xiii
    L. Diane Bernard

Preface   xv
    Natalie Jane Woodman

Introduction: Lesbians of Color–A Kaleidoscope   1
    Hilda Hidalgo

For the White Social Worker Who Wants to Know
    how to Work with Lesbians of Color   7
    Mary E. Swigonski

The Norms of Conduct in Social Service Agencies:
    A Threat to the Mental Health of Puerto Rican Lesbians   23
    Hilda Hidalgo

Whose Daughter Are You? Exploring Identity Issues
    of Lesbians Who Are Adopted   43
    Mi Ok Bruining

A Few Thoughts from a Korean, Adopted, Lesbian,
    Writer/Poet, and Social Worker   61
    Mi Ok Bruining

The Social Service Needs of Lesbians of Color   67
    Mary E. Swigonski

Lesbian Latinas: Organizational Efforts to End Oppression   85
    Mariana Romo-Carmona

Being Pro-Gay and Pro-Lesbian in Straight Institutions   95
    Cheryl Clarke

Index   101

ABOUT THE EDITOR

Hilda Hidalgo, PhD, is Professor Emerita at Rutgers University and serves on the editorial board of the *Journal of Gay & Lesbian Psychotherapy.* She is a member of the Advisory Committee of the New Jersey Department of Human Services, the National Association of Social Workers, and the Association of College and University Professors. She founded and was first president of Aspira, Inc., of New Jersey and of the State of New Jersey Puerto Rican Congress. Dr. Hidalgo has published several articles and addressed numerous conferences on topics including Hispanics in higher education, Puerto Ricans in New Jersey, and gay and lesbian issues. She is a certified marriage counselor, certified teacher, and certified with the Academy of Certified Social Workers and the Academy of Certified Clinical Social Workers.

Foreword

To encounter Hilda Hidalgo is like being exposed to fine crystal—
  her voice rings with utter clarity
The analogy, while true, is limited by association with fragility
  when, in fact, her power is strong and forceful
Passionate and compassionate by turn: both courageous and outra-
  geous
She is and has been a true lesbian warrior.

Long before it was chic or politically correct
  she was not only out, but outspoken
In exposing the corrosive effect of homophobia
For more than a quarter of a century she has taken
  personal and professional risks to combat
  all forms of oppression and injustice toward women
Her voice has been consistently heard in behalf of
  lesbians of color suffering multiple discriminations.
It is a tribute to her outstanding leadership and consistent
  contributions that she was invited to edit
  this special collection
There could be no better choice.

L. Diane Bernard, PhD

L. Diane Bernard, PhD, is currently enjoying her recently claimed retirement, and continues to serve as a consultant to schools of social work. She has served as Acting Director of the Council on Social Work Education, Dean of the School of Social Work of Florida State University, and Director of the Doctoral Program at Virginia Commonwealth University, Richmond.

Her address is 5623 Gulf Drive, Panama City Beach, FL 32408.

[Haworth co-indexing entry note]: "Foreword." Bernard, L. Diane. Co-published simultaneously in *Journal of Gay & Lesbian Social Services* (The Haworth Press, Inc.) Vol. 3, No. 2, 1995, p. xv; and: *Lesbians of Color: Social and Human Services* (ed: Hilda Hidalgo) The Haworth Press, Inc., 1995, p. xiii; and: *Lesbians of Color: Social and Human Services* (ed: Hilda Hidalgo) Harrington Park Press, an imprint of The Haworth Press, Inc., 1995, p. xiii. Multiple copies of this article/chapter may be purchased from The Haworth Document Delivery Center [1-800-3-HAWORTH; 9:00 a.m. - 5:00 p.m. (EST)].

Preface

It has been with feelings of great honor and privilege that I have read this significant collection of articles by lesbian women of color. In searches of recent Annotated Bibliographies (Epstein & Zak, 1992; Lee, 1991), one becomes only too aware of the paucity of social work writing related specifically to *women* who are *lesbian* and who are *from diverse ethnic groups*. As a social work pioneer publishing in this area, it is fitting that Hilda Hidalgo should be the editor of this special collection, contributing her own wisdom and drawing together a unique group of lesbian writers to provide "decibels of sound for a community whose voice had been so feeble in our social work literature." Each author provides knowledge, practical (as in social work practice) and attitudinal insights to enhance our interactions with lesbians of color.

The "Multicultural Lesbian Publication" is not limited in focus but, for the first time, speaks to special issues of lesbians of color: adoption, class differences, physical challenge, and mental health issues. The personalized accounts from various authors graphically depict the deep-seated impacts of racism, sexism, and homophobia in our society. When coupled with the scholarship derived from "different ways of knowing," this body of work guides us to operationalize the profession's Code of Ethics so well that we all may

---

Natalie Jane Woodman, ACSW, CISW, is Professor Emerita, Arizona State University School of Social Work. She has published extensively in both social work and lesbian and gay studies. She continues to contribute to the lesbian and gay community through counseling, consultation, and writing.

[Haworth co-indexing entry note]: "Preface." Woodman, Natalie Jane. Co-published simultaneously in *Journal of Gay & Lesbian Social Services* (The Haworth Press, Inc.) Vol. 3, No. 2, 1995, pp. xvii-xxi; and: *Lesbians of Color: Social and Human Services* (ed: Hilda Hidalgo) The Haworth Press, Inc., 1995, pp. xv-xix; and: *Lesbians of Color: Social and Human Services* (ed: Hilda Hidalgo) Harrington Park Press, an imprint of The Haworth Press, Inc., 1995, pp. xv-xix. Multiple copies of this article/chapter may be purchased from The Haworth Document Delivery Center [1-800-3-HAWORTH; 9:00 a.m. - 5:00 p.m. (EST)].

xv

become models for social change and social justice. It also guides us in our respect for difference and our mandate to end oppression.

Notable themes throughout the articles include: feminism as a pervasive model for empowerment; empowerment as a tool for healing; healing as an alternative for victimization; using the power of words for exorcising the demons of racism, homophobia, and all the other "isms"; social change as the overriding goal of social work if we are to move from oppression to self-actualization for all; and, perhaps most crucially, the application of "Standpoint Theory" to practice and to our very lives. Internalizing new Standpoints permits the reader to move from intellectual to empathic grasp of the point made by each author. Another very significant contribution by the authors is the inclusion of a breadth of references related to lesbians of color. The readings proposed are not only scholarly but emotionally touching and/or just plain fun.

Following Hidalgo's introductory delineation of common themes addressing oppression and her definition of Standpoint Theory, Swigonski opens the volume with clear identification of the trinity of awareness, knowledge and skills needed by social workers in interaction with lesbians of color. Her sensitive and scholarly presentation challenges the reader to become open to alternative and non-traditional ways of learning from clients and colleagues if we are to become effective persons and helping professionals. The perception that we can and must suspend our own cultural biases and ethnocentric stances if we are to be truly empathic has far-reaching implications for all levels of practice. So, too, does Swigonski's charge to learn to recognize and *use* differences from "loving perception."

Hidalgo provides an articulate presentation of what I call a "crazy-making world" arising from institutionalized homophobia reflected in the current "don't ask, don't tell" oppression. The need to maintain dichotomous public and private selves is not only a base for fear (and sometimes actual terror) but also can be a source for development of true anomie. Hidalgo demonstrates some of the mental health issues most graphically in her interview with a social work colleague. This very courageous young friend demonstrates the insanity of double talk, double messages (overt versus covert racism and homophobia), and double lives for lesbians of color.

However, more vitally, they give to the reader the hope and beauty of the power of the human spirit of women who transcend social injustice to become not just survivors, but "thrivers."

The transcendence over oppression is represented very graphically in the documentation of coping with loss, abandonment, racism, sexism, and homophobia encountered by many adopted persons. Mi Ok Bruining adds new "standpoints" for our awareness as she identifies yet another level of subordination that comes with infantilizing adult lesbian women who are still classified as "adopted children" well into their later years! The author also gives new meaning to identity development and coming out processes for those lesbian women who are still grappling with issues stemming from the adoption process. The "coming out steps" with which we are so familiar indeed grossly neglected the ramifications of coming out for women of color–who struggle with potential cultural taboos and rejection from nurturing systems which have been buffers against the racism in the sustaining environmental institutions. Now envision the complex coming out process which involves the closets of both one's lesbian-identified world *and* the more frustrating "adoptee" identity. Bruining's poetic herstory truly reflects progression from feeling loss to experiencing anger to "letting the anger go" and moving on to self-actualization. How privileged we are to have her sharing this growth with us.

In Swigonski's second article–this one identifying differences in perceptions of social service needs between lesbian women of color and other lesbian/gay persons–what stands out is the strength of women in coping with many oppressions and surviving "under the worst conditions." Once more, we are confronted with the refusal to accept status as victims. Once more we are challenged to move from positions of power to identify *issues* (not "ranking" oppressions) and engage in *social change*. Lesbian women of color demonstrate their increased frustration with and attention to societal injustice–directing our attention to the complex array of problems crying for solution.

Romo-Carmona describes for the reader the priorities which historically have demanded attention from lesbian women of color (primarily racism and economic marginalization). Additionally, she depicts the emerging change from having put lesbian identity on a back shelf to affirming this important dimension of self. Once more we see optimism, resource identification, use of visibility to confront social consciousness in others, and the ever present charge to effect social change.

Clarke, from her vantage point as a mid-years "black, queer, feminist, and marvelous" woman, looks at both past encounters and current perceptions of the empowerment that came with experiences related to her multiple identities. Once more, optimism and transcendence are themes that pervade the author's approach to being a lesbian woman of color. However, lest we become sanguine, Clarke also reenforces the need to challenge the status quo. More than other contributors to this volume, she perceives identity as a political choice as well as an opportunity for developing new strategies to impact the bastions of power, racism, sexism, and homophobia. Furthermore, Clarke brings home the point that "straight human service providers have almost as much at stake as queer human service providers, particularly as we face the anti-sex beliefs, practices, and discourses that have such virulent currency at present." To this I would add the theme of all the women writers–white lesbian women, white gay men, and gay men of all colors all have as much at stake as lesbian women of color and have as much responsibility to move toward implementing social change. Indeed, "when one of us is oppressed (much less oppressed from multiple sources), we all are oppressed."

The social work profession owes a debt of gratitude to the women who have contributed to this book. They have shown courage in a time of vicious backlash. They have shown exceptional levels of risk-taking in the face of potential emotional, physical, and economic loss from those who will not laud the beauty of their lives and the poetry of their words. They have given us challenges for our own development–as individuals, as professionals facing our code of ethics, as fellow travellers journeying toward ever increasing capabilities to view our world and the worlds of others from continuously changing "standpoints," and as potential agents for social change.

Natalie Jane Woodman, ACSW, CISW

REFERENCES

Epstein, A. L. & Zak, P. D. (1992). *The master of social work core curriculum: Inclusion of gay, lesbian and bisexual content: An annotated bibliography.* San Francisco: 2265 15th Street (Self Publisher).

Lee, J. A. B. (1991). *An annotated bibliography of gay and lesbian readings.* East Rockaway, N. Y.: Cummings & Hathaway.

Introduction:
Lesbians of Color–A Kaleidoscope

The last decade is viewed by many as a landmark in the struggle of lesbians and gay men to remove from the institutions of society the prejudices and misconceptions (including those that claimed a research or scientific base) that labeled all lesbians and gay men as sick, maladjusted, immoral. The label, in turn, justified social institutions' actions in making and enforcing laws, protocols of treatment and administrative rules and practices that oppressed those so labeled. Institutionalized oppression of gay men and lesbians is as prevalent in America as racism and sexism, with the difference that many corrective steps have been incorporated in the laws to prevent blatant and law-supported discrimination on the basis of race and gender.

In the late sixties "closeted" professionals who had gained respectability and credibility in their professions "came out of the closet" and started processes and organizational efforts to end the oppression of and discrimination against gay men and lesbians in social institutions and professions. At the forefront of these movements were social workers and psychologists.

In 1973, the American Psychiatric Association removed homosexuality from the list of mental disorders, and that same year the American Public Health Association deplored all public and private discrimination against lesbians and gay men. In 1977 the National Association of Social Workers (N.A.S.W.) affirmed the rights of all

[Haworth co-indexing entry note]: "Introduction." Hidalgo, Hilda. Co-published simultaneously in *Journal of Gay & Lesbian Social Services* (The Haworth Press, Inc.) Vol. 3, No. 2, 1995, pp. 1-5; and: *Lesbians of Color: Social and Human Services* (ed: Hilda Hidalgo) The Haworth Press, Inc., 1995, pp. 1-5; and: *Lesbians of Color: Social and Human Services* (ed: Hilda Hidalgo) Harrington Park Press, an imprint of The Haworth Press, Inc., 1995, pp. 1-5. Multiple copies of this article/chapter may be purchased from The Haworth Document Delivery Center [1-800-3-HAWORTH; 9:00 a.m. - 5:00 p.m. (EST)].

1

persons to define and express their own sexuality, "and vowed to" combat laws and other forms of discrimination which impose less than equal status upon the homosexual members of the human family. The organized movement within professional organizations, led by gay men and lesbian members of the professional organizations, gained steam and lesbian and gay organized groups are active today in almost all professional organizations that provide human services. These include organizations of lawyers, teachers, law enforcement officers, physicians, nurses, librarians and leaders of all major religious organizations.

Professional journals, books, research studies, and media presentations began addressing lesbians and gay men from assumptions and perspectives that were not based in the old paradigms of viewing homosexual behavior and homosexual orientation as intrinsically abnormal, deprived, sinful, and unhealthy.

Publications that addressed homosexual and bisexual concerns exclusively and from the new non-pathological assumption entered the family of legitimate professional literature. Among these was the *Journal of Gay & Lesbian Social Services.*

By 1980, the voices and experiences of gay men and lesbians were no longer absent or invisible in the professional literature of the disciplines that help shape the practice of professionals in the human service arena. However, the voices, perspectives, and research were still predominantly anchored in a white, eurocentric, male perspective . . . a perspective that was valid when applied to the racial, ethnic, and gender group that shaped and validated its conclusions and recommendations. A perspective anchored in the experience of lesbians of color has been only sparsely represented in professional publications. (A literature search using the library computer catalog of Rutgers University in all journals in the human services professions and disciplines from 1980 to the present, and using as code lesbians, Afro-American, Hispanic and Asian, produced a total of only thirty-eight (38) citations.) The voice and experience of lesbians of color is still a mostly absent voice in the literature at a time when their presence as clients of social service agencies is at an all-time high.

When I was asked to be editor for this publication, I saw it as an opportunity to add some decibels of sound for a community whose voice had been so feeble in our social service literature. I wanted that voice to come directly from lesbians of color, amplified by a *Standpoint* approach (Collins, 1986, 1989, 1990; Harding, 1991; McCarl-Nilsen, 1990) that could offer human service professionals a different way of gaining insight and understanding, and a springboard for valuing and celebrating the experience and perspectives of lesbians of color so that social service professionals, in turn, could provide more effective services to members of this population.

Standpoint involves a level of conscious awareness about one's social location and that location's relation to one's lived experience. *Standpoint theory* begins with the idea that the less powerful members of society experience a *different reality* as a consequence of their oppression. Lesbians of color who experience multiple levels of oppression interpret reality as a consequence of this oppression. Theirs is an interpretation that is different not only from that of the dominant group, but also from that of lesbians and gay men who have only experienced oppression based on their sexual and/or gender orientation.

In order to survive, subordinate persons must be aware of (and often accommodate to) the perspective of the dominant class as well as their own. This gives lesbians of color the potential for a more complete and complex view of social reality. The fact that we lesbians of color see reality with a multi-faceted perspective, filtered through the prisms of multiple realities, is not intended to deny or make glamorous the consequences of oppression.

As an activist in many fronts of the struggle to end oppression and discrimination based on the model of a "preferred sameness" (read: white, male, heterosexist, eurocentric, middle class, body-able, professional, between the ages of mid-twenties to early fifty), I welcomed the opportunity and the freedom given me to examine the realities of lesbians of color within the theme of the kaleidoscope metaphor. The kaleidoscope metaphor is representative of the diversity present in the lives and culture of lesbians of color. It reflects how individuals put together in different configurations the many pieces of their life experience in a manner that is constantly evolving, and that reflects new and ever changing visions to each other.

Calls for submission of papers for this volume were sent to a variety of lesbian professional groups, feminist professional groups, and mainstream professional organizations, as well as to the more "underground" network of lesbians of color. The articles selected for publication in this collection are the results of this outreach effort. In the process, I learned that there is a reluctance on the part of lesbians of color to invest professional expertise in an issue that from their "standpoint" will bring few if any professional rewards and may present some professional liabilities. My optimistic perceptions, based on the progress of acceptance of lesbians in the human service profession, were apparently not shared by the majority of the professional lesbians of color who remain mostly in the closet. I also learned that, despite those few of us who have survived "out of the closet" in our professional careers, there is a vast majority of sisters and brothers who view coming out professionally as sudden death. Yet, considering the "small deaths" suffered each day in the lives of so many lesbians and gay men, we must recognize and celebrate the courage expressed in each step they take to contribute to wider understanding of their unique perspectives, and to build the hope of more humane and insightful actions to meet their needs.

All seven articles included here were written by lesbians and all but two were written by lesbians of color. While differing in focus and approach, all seven articles share some *common themes* which are basic to:

1. The multi-oppression of lesbians of color, and the effects of these interlocking oppressions in daily life, in the workplace, and in the development of self-identity and self-worth.

   Some of these oppressions are shared by both lesbians and gay men, but are often differently applied and experienced. Most studies have focused almost exclusively on gay men and we cannot automatically assume that the findings of these studies apply to lesbians. Almost no studies have examined the perspectives of lesbians of color.

2. *Heterosexist assumptions that are perceived and intertwined with racism, sexism and classism throughout* the structure, norms and protocols of human service (and other) institutions and agencies.

Heterosexism–institutionalized and ideologically dominant in our society–is oppressive to *all* women, straight *and* lesbian. A symbiotic relationship exists between heterosexism and the perpetuation of the power and oppression by the patriarchy.

3. The fallacy and dangers of separating the "public" and the "private" aspects of lesbian (and gay) lives (e.g., in the workplace), and evidence of the ways in which this commonly held distinction can prevent liberation, and self-actualization and how following the dictates of the public/private dichotomy affects an individual's mental health.

4. *Standpoint/Standpoint Theory,* which can be effectively used to help change the way we construct our social institutions.

Each of these articles uses "standpoint" theory, not only to help the reader view life via the eyes of lesbians of color, but also to aid the reader's own use of standpoint as an instrument of individual and social empowerment and a guide to more humane and effective social work practice.

"Standpoint" is offered as a way to not only walk in other's shoes–but to move closer to experience-generated feelings–others and our own.

Hilda Hidalgo, PhD, ACSW
Newark, NJ

REFERENCES

Collins, P. H. (1986). Learning from the outsider within: The sociological significance of Black feminist thought. *Social Problems, 33* (6), 514-532.

Collins, P. H. (1989). The social construction of Black feminist thought. *Signs 11* (4), 745-773.

Collins, P. H. (1990). *Black feminist thought: Knowledge, consciousness, and the politics of empowerment.* London, UK: Harper Collins Academic.

Harding, S. (1991). *Whose science? Whose knowledge? Thinking from women's lives.* New York: Cornell University Press.

McCarl-Nilsen, J. (Ed.). (1990). *Feminist research methods: Exemplary readings in the social sciences.* Boulder, CO: Westview Press.

For the White Social Worker
Who Wants to Know
how to Work with Lesbians of Color

Mary E. Swigonski

SUMMARY. This article challenges white social workers who want to work effectively with lesbians of color to identify the patterns of privilege and to step outside of those patterns. Three layers of competence for practice with lesbians of color are described: awareness, knowledge, and skill. Awareness includes attitudes related to racism, sexism, heterosexism, and homophobia. Knowledge about lesbians of color is developed from their standpoint. Skills include the ability to deal with the multiple issues involved in "coming out," being women of color, being lesbian, experiencing transitional and environmental crises; identifying appropriate resources; and empowering lesbians of color to alleviate oppression.

"the first thing you must do is forget that I'm a lesbian of color;
second you must never forget that I'm a lesbian of color"
(to rephrase Pat Parker's poem "To the white person who wants
to know how to be my friend," 1990, p. 297).

Mary E. Swigonski, PhD, ACSW, is Assistant Professor, Social Work Department, Rutgers, The State University of New Jersey Campus at Newark, 360 Dr. Martin Luther King Jr. Blvd., Newark, NJ 07102. Her research interests include feminist standpoint theory and its implications for social work research and for practice and program evaluation.

[Haworth co-indexing entry note]: "For the White Social Worker Who Wants to Know how to Work with Lesbians of Color." Swigonski, Mary E. Co-published simultaneously in *Journal of Gay & Lesbian Social Services* (The Haworth Press, Inc.) Vol. 3, No. 2, 1995, pp. 7-21; and: *Lesbians of Color: Social and Human Services* (ed: Hilda Hidalgo) The Haworth Press, Inc., 1995, pp. 7-21; and: *Lesbians of Color: Social and Human Services* (ed: Hilda Hidalgo) Harrington Park Press, an imprint of The Haworth Press, Inc., 1995, pp. 7-21. Multiple copies of this article/chapter may be purchased from The Haworth Document Delivery Center [1-800-3-HAWORTH; 9:00 a.m. - 5:00 p.m. (EST)].

7

In her poem, Parker advises the white person who wants to be her friend to be knowledgeable about her (African-American) culture without trying to be more knowledgeable than Parker; to enjoy her culture, without expecting Parker to provide the entertainment; to be aware of prejudices, without apologizing to Parker for them. Parker identifies a pattern of assumed privilege and superiority, and challenges the white person who would be her friend to step outside of that pattern. That is an appropriate challenge for white (lesbian, gay, or heterosexual) social workers who want to work effectively with lesbians of color.

White social workers can begin this process by understanding the social location of lesbians of color. Lesbians of color live their lives at the intersection of three cultures: the culture of their ethnic group, the culture of lesbians, and the culture of white society. Social work practice with lesbians of color is profoundly multicultural social work practice. Pederson (1988) describes a three-stage process of developing multicultural competence: awareness, knowledge, and skill. This paper applies and expands Pederson's three stages of developing multicultural competence for practice with lesbians of color.

AWARENESS

For Pederson, awareness includes an understanding of one's assumptions about differences and similarities of behavior, attitudes, and values. When working with lesbians of color, it is important for practitioners to be aware of their attitudes related to internalized racism, internalized sexism, internalized heterosexism, and internalized homophobia. It is similarly important to be aware of the differing forms and characteristics that these oppressions embody. For example, Hoagland (1988) notes that people of color have been oppressed through the perpetuation of a set of social beliefs about their inferiority, the belief that they are culturally disadvantaged, deprived, or backwards. These beliefs have been used to justify the enslavement and economic exploitation of people of color. The lands of Native Americans were stolen, and they were relegated to reservations. Women's identities are defined as lives subordinated to men, the dominant members of society. Hoagland makes the point that all of these forms of oppression are defined in terms of a relationship to the dominant culture. However, lesbian oppression is not primarily a form of relationship. Lesbians are oppressed by having their existence erased and denied.

Lesbians simply do not exist in society. Hoagland (1988) explains that lesbians, when they are discussed, are described as women who hate men, as a phase in a heterosexual woman's life, as women who cannot get men, as a man in a woman's body: lesbians are a deviant form of something else. The idea of a woman simply loving a woman is inconceivable within the dominant social construction. It threatens the social order. The idea of a woman loving a woman and being able to survive without men usurps men's access to women. Lesbians' lives deny men access to certain females, which substantially cuts off a flow of benefits (female caregiving) to them. It is an assumption of power. Understood from the mind set of this system of oppression, lesbians of color are inferior women, who fail to fulfill their caregiving responsibilities to men, and who usurp men's power. These are some of the assumptions that found the social order that requires universal heterosexuality.

Heterosexism is a political force as well as a sexual preference (Bunch, 1978). Heterosexism is also a cognitive posture. Lesbianism is also a political force, sexual orientation, and cognitive posture.

Heterosexism is the institutionalized and ideological domination of heterosexuality. Heterosexism requires a pattern of relationships in which men dominate women. Heterosexism conditions cognition based on either/or dualities that support patterns of domination and subordination.

Lesbianism is an orientation of a woman's life around women, woman identification, and a commitment to women as a political force capable of changing society. Lesbianism, as a sexual orientation, invites the redefinition of relationships between women. Lesbianism, as a cognitive posture, invites divergent thinking, the movement away from set patterns and goals, toward a more whole perspective, one that includes rather than excludes (Anzaldua, 1987, p. 79).

Heterosexism is a way of life that is enforced by every formal institution of the dominant society. It is a way of living that normalizes the domination of one person, and the subordination of another. Lesbianism is a way of life that is denied by every formal institution of the dominant society because it challenges the hegemony of society's structures.

Racism, sexism, heterosexism, and classism are pervasive throughout the social structure. These oppressions are interlocking, and interdependent. Greater attention has been given to the nature of heterosexist oppression in this paper, not because it is the primary oppression (it is not), but because it is the least visible oppression.

To become aware of one's attitudes regarding particular oppressions, it is helpful to learn to understand oneself as both a victim and a perpetrator of oppression. This is difficult because we live in a society that emphasizes either/or dichotomous world views (Anzaldua, 1987, 1990a, 1990b; Minh-ha, 1990). We live our lives making either/or choices. Learning to look at oneself from this both/and position gives new dimension to self-understanding. Looking at oneself from only one dimension loses the awareness of the many times that one participates in maintaining a system that distributes rewards based on age, gender, class, sexual orientation, religious and cultural background, physical and mental abilities. Each person participates in that system through a variety of day-to-day activities. Actions that do not work to effect the transformation (or sabotage) of the system of subordination and unearned privileges, participate in, and support the oppression.

In developing one's awareness of behaviors and attitudes related to these forms of oppression, it is also helpful to develop an awareness of the gains and privileges that accrue to oppressors. Each person, at different moments, is both the oppressor and the oppressed. It is easier for social workers with a commitment to social justice, to recognize the forms of oppression that constrain their lives. It is more difficult, but vitally important, to develop an awareness of the unearned advantages that accrue within one's life simply by virtue of membership in a particular group, the often invisible privileges that are the secondary gains of oppression. That understanding helps to clarify the ways that each person oppresses others (intentionally or not).

Privileges are pervasive throughout each person's life. They are frequently invisible to the person who enjoys them. Privileges are quite visible to those to whom they are denied. For example, Anzaldua (1990a, 1990b) notes that people of color are treated generically by the dominant culture (as in this article); this forces persons of color to experience themselves collectively. As a result, persons of color are called on to speak for, and are held responsible for, the whole of their group. Whites, however, are not named white, because that is the taken-for-granted norm. Whites are not held accountable for all whites; their individuality is virtually guaranteed.

Writing this article in terms of lesbians of color reflects white privilege. It would be far more precise and accurate to frame these considerations in terms of the unique needs and circumstances of each particular group of lesbians of color: of Latina lesbians, Chicana lesbians, Puerto Rican lesbians, Cuban lesbians, South American lesbians, African American lesbians, Asian-Pacific Island lesbians, Native lesbians, not to mention each of the unique countries that these groupings obscure. White privilege allows the blurring of the uniqueness of each of these groups within this article, and throughout our collective awareness.

Some of the privileges that accrue from membership in the heterosexual group include social and family acceptance, economic security, and male legitimacy (Bunch, 1978). Bunch also notes that legal and physical protection are more generously available to heterosexuals. The degree to which an individual receives these benefits depends upon her or his race, sex, class, and how much that person plays by the dominant culture's rules. Through heterosexual privilege, a woman is given a stake in behaving properly, or in the case of a lesbian, pretending to behave properly, and thus maintaining the system that perpetuates her own oppression. Bunch cautions, however, that heterosexual privileges are not lasting benefits or power, but are small short-term bribes, meted out in return for giving up lasting self-discovery and collective power. She further asserts that ultimately freedom and empowerment depend less on society's acceptance, than on changing its basic tenets.

To practice effectively with lesbians of color, social workers need to be aware of how their beliefs and attitudes are shaped by the assumptions that ground these forms of oppression. Social workers need to become aware of the privileges that accrue within their lives as a result of the ways that they (consciously or not) oppress others. In order to work effectively with lesbians of color, and not to further contribute to their oppression, social workers need to have a clear sense of who they are, how their prejudices get reinforced, and how they create institutions to reenact those collective prejudices (Molina, 1990). Understanding personal and institutional power is a primary task in the process of liberation. For social workers, a necessary first step is self-examination: self-examination of attitudes and beliefs about oppressed groups; of the privileges in one's life; of one's access to and use of personal and institutional power. This first step grounds an education about "facts," and a commitment to moral responsibility to end oppression (Woodman, 1989).

KNOWLEDGE

Knowledge acquisition expands one's information about culturally learned assumptions (Pederson, 1988). In order to practice effectively with lesbians of color, social workers also need to develop their knowledge about lesbians of color. But, the existing social order defines lesbians of color as inferior beings, who abrogate their social responsibilities to meet the needs of men. For effective practice with lesbians of color, social workers must find an alternative source of knowledge. Knowledge developed from the standpoint of lesbians of color is a powerful alternative source of information.

Arrogant perceptions (perceptions that generate characterizations like the earlier definition of lesbians of color) are the result of knowledge that fails to identify with persons one views or has come to see as the product of that perception (Lugones, 1990). Flexibility in shifting from the mainstream construction of life to other constructions of life, helps to avoid arrogant perceptions. This flexibility is necessary for persons whose lives are outside the dominant culture (lesbians of color); it is a survival strategy. This kind of flexibility can also be learned and willfully exercised by those who are at ease in the mainstream society (white heterosexual social workers, for example).

Lugones refers to the ability to shift one's standpoint, or view of reality, to other constructions, as perceiving others lovingly. To accomplish loving perception, it is necessary to consult something other than one's own will, interests, fears, or imagination. What needs to be consulted is the reality as seen with the eyes of the other. What is necessary is to enter into her world, to see us both as we are constructed in her world, and to witness her own sense of herself from within her world. Understood within the context of social work practice, Lugones has provided a profoundly powerful description of empathic understanding. Understood within the context of social work practice with lesbians of color, this invites social workers to become cognitive lesbians (to think divergently, to move away from set patterns and goals, toward a more whole perspective, toward a perspective that includes rather than excludes differing day-to-day realities) in order to achieve empathy with lesbians of color.

This kind of identification with others can result in a distinct interpretation and understanding of differing social realities. Scholars have long recognized the tendency toward enmeshment in the relationships of lesbians (of all colors) (see, for example, Krestan & Bepko, 1980). Much professional work has focused on helping lesbians to overcome this tendency and to attain independence and autonomy within relationships. In contrast, Audre Lorde looks at the relationships between lesbians with the kind of loving identification that Lugones is describing. Lorde (1981) reinterprets the need and desire for women to nurture each other not as pathological, but as redemptive. It is within that knowledge that our real power is discovered. It is this real connection that is feared by the patriarchal world. Lorde further observes that interdependence between women is the only way to the freedom for the "I" to "be," not in order to be used, but to be creative.

Through traveling to the world of a lesbian of color, a social worker will be able to identify with her. To rephrase Lugones' (1990) description of the outcomes of the process of loving perception, only then will practitioners cease to ignore lesbians of color. Only then will practitioners begin to be able to see lesbians of color as subjects, even if subjected. Only then will social workers see how meaning can arise fully between the two. In traveling to the world of the other we become dependent on each other for the possibility of being understood. Without this kind of traveling to the world of each other, we are not intelligible to each other. Without knowing the other's world, without knowing the dailyness of the others' life, social workers do not know lesbians of color. Audre Lorde (1982) emphasizes the importance of this kind of world traveling and loving perception in her comment that in the recognition of loving lies an answer to despair.

Alarcon (1990) stresses the importance of developing knowledge from the standpoint of lesbians of color, with her comment that the power of white-anglo women over women of color is in inverse proportion to their working knowledge of each other. She notes that because of their lack of knowledge, white women who try to enter into a dialogue with women of color inevitably interrupt this dialogue. Before European-American social workers can contribute to the dialogue with lesbians of color, they need to know the text. They need to become familiar with alternative ways of viewing the world. European-American social workers need to learn to "become unintrusive, unimportant, patient to the point of tears, while at the same time open to learning any possible lessons" (Alarcon, 1990, p. 363). European-American social workers will have to come to terms with a sense of alienation, of not belonging, of having their world thoroughly disrupted, of having it criticized and scrutinized, from the point of view of those who have been harmed by it, and being viewed with distrust.

The development of loving knowledge about lesbians of color (in their own terms) can then lead to the development of knowledge about the nature of our differences. Difference, whether it is sexual, racial, class or social, has to be conceptualized within a political and ideological domain (Alarcon, 1990). Difference does not necessarily give rise to separatism (Minh-ha, 1990). Difference is not what makes conflict; difference is beyond and alongside conflict. Many social workers still hold on to the concept of difference, not as a tool of creativity with which to question multiple forms of repression and dominance, but as a tool of segregation, to exert power on the basis of racial and sexual essences. Learning to use difference as a tool of creativity, to question and transform the multiple forms of repression and dominance, is a powerful opportunity.

Our refusal to recognize, accept, and celebrate our differences keeps us apart (Molina, 1990). "We have started to recognize our differences. We have named them. We have analyzed their constructions. However, we have a harder time accepting and celebrating them. We live in a society where sameness is venerated as the most desirable quality" (Molina, 1990, p. 333). It takes an act of loving perception to recognize, accept and celebrate our differences. Lorde (1981, p. 99) points out that "difference must not be merely tolerated, but must be seen as a fund of necessary polarities between which our creativity can spark like a dialectic. Only then does the necessity for interdependence become unthreatening. Only within that interdependency of different strengths, acknowledged and equal, can the power to seek new ways to actively 'be' in the world generate, as well as the courage and sustenance to act where there are no charters . . . Difference is that raw and powerful connection from which our personal power is forged." We have been taught to ignore our differences, to view them as causes for separation and suspicion, rather than as forces for growth, creativity, and change.

From within this standpoint, social workers need to develop their knowledge about four aspects of the reality of the lives of lesbians of color: the history of their oppression, their history of resistance and change efforts, their unique strengths, and the ways in which their unique standpoint can transform perceptions of social reality.

Far too much social science theory and knowledge still describes the modal person as a self-sufficient individual adult (who is still a white man). As a result of this focus on modal, average persons, lesbians of color are readily excluded from social science knowledge. We have not yet explored how our understanding of gender relations, self, and theory are partially constituted in and through experiences of living in a culture in which asymmetrical race, gender, and class relations are central organizing principles of the society (Alarcon, 1990). Knowledge production needs to be transformed to a celebration of difference, rather than an erasure of it.

Approaching knowledge through the celebration of difference leads one to question the myths and misinformation transmitted by the dominant culture. For this approach to knowledge, documents in which lesbians of color speak for themselves, in their own words, are important sources of information. These include oral histories, diaries, interviews, and first person written narratives. Appended to the end of this article is a brief resource list of anthologies containing such works by lesbians of color.

Those involved in knowledge production, and those involved in working with multicultural clients need to develop what Anzaldua (1990) calls a Mestiza consciousness. Mestiza consciousness is the ability to synthesize differences through acts of self-definition and rebellion. This approach to consciousness leads to a path of knowledge, one of knowing and learning. Those involved in knowledge production, and those involved in working with multicultural clients need to become cognitive lesbians, women committed to the loving knowledge of women. By knowing and learning through multiple processes, social workers can help lesbians of color to construct their own identities. This kind of knowing leads to unmasking one's subjectivity as well as interlacing experiences, with strategies and with theories that strengthen and support women of color. This kind of knowledge leads to action.

SKILL

For effective multicultural social work, Pederson (1988) highlights the need to adapt effective and efficient actions with people of different cultures. This adaptation emerges from the knowledge of the other's social reality that the author described above. Effective multicultural social work practice requires transforming traditional approaches to practice based on what has been learned. Kanuha (1990) identifies the path for skill development, in her description of skillful social work practice with lesbians of color. She indicates that in dealing with the issues presented by lesbians of color, social workers need to confront the issues presented by clearly delineating the multiple issues involved in "coming out" about being women of color and being lesbian; experience the transitional and environmental crises that inhabit the dailyness of their lives, along with identifying appropriate responses and resources to each of those situations; and empower lesbians of color to alleviate the domination and oppression throughout their lives.

In order to work effectively with lesbians of color, social workers need to develop skills not only in effective interpersonal practice, but also in building alliances with lesbians of color, both individually and as groups. Alliance work is the attempt to shift positions, to reposition ourselves regarding our individual identities (Anzaldua, 1990). Anzaldua notes that in doing alliance work, we are confronted with problems of how we share or don't share space, how we position our individual selves with other individuals or groups who are different from and at odds with each other. Lesbians of color, who are members of multiple and conflicting groups, must reconcile their love for those diverse groups when members of those groups do not love each other, cannot relate to each other, and do not know how to work together. She reminds us that alliance work stirs up intimacy issues, and issues of trust.

Alliance work attempts to balance power relations and to undermine and subvert the system of domination and subordination. It is important when doing this work to remember that we live in a world where whites dominate people of color. We participate in that system every minute of our lives.

Those doing alliance work may all be in the same water, but we are in different boats. This makes it particularly important to agree to the terms of participation in constructing alliances. When alliances don't collectively define themselves and the terms of their work, the group will automatically operate under the assumptions, definitions, and strategies which prevail in the dominant society. Those are the assumptions, definitions and strategies that support the systems of oppression and not empowerment. In building alliances and coalitions with lesbians of color, social workers have frequently invited lesbians of color to join us and give us input. At least that tells them that we know they exist. It is time, however, to join lesbians of color in their struggle, rather than having them join us in our struggles (Yamada, 1981). It is time to join with lesbians of color in their work for empowerment.

Solomon (1976) has identified four goals of social work from an empowerment perspective. Those goals include helping the client perceive:

1. herself as a causal agent in achieving a solution to her problems;
2. the practitioner as having knowledge and skills that the client can use;
3. the practitioner as peer-collaborator or partner in the problem-solving effort;

4. the "power structure" as multipolar, demonstrating varying degrees of commitment to the status quo and therefore open to influence (Solomon, 1976, p. 26).

Working from an empowerment perspective, social workers can help lesbians of color to understand that they are not hated and abused because there is something wrong with them, but because their status and treatment are prescribed by the racist, sexist, misogynistic, heterosexist system under which we live (Smith, 1983). An empowering social work practice will understand that it is not something that lesbians of color have done that has heaped this psychic violence and material abuse upon them. It is rather the very fact that, because of who they are, they are multiply oppressed. An empowering social work practice will then work with lesbians of color to use that understanding to transform the social structure.

Effective social work practice with lesbians of color will trouble the social structure. As Judith Butler (1990) suggests, trouble need not carry a negative valence. Defining trouble as something negative is the ruse of the power structure. Butler's analysis of the process through which the prevailing social structure uses trouble as a threat develops along this line: one is threatened with trouble, one is even put in trouble, all to keep one out of trouble. Using this logic, trouble is inevitable. If that is true, then the task for the white social worker who wants to know how to work with lesbians of color is how to best make trouble in consort with lesbians of color, and what way to be in it together.

REFERENCES

Alarcon, N. (1990). The theoretical subject(s) of *This bridge called my back* and Anglo-American feminism. In G. Anzaldua (Ed.). *Making face, making soul/ haciendo caras: Creative and critical perspectives by women of color* (pp. 356-369). San Francisco: Aunt Lute Foundation.

Anzaldua, G. (1987). *Borderlands/la frontera: The new mestiza.* San Francisco: Spinsters/Aunt Lute Foundation.

Anzaldua, G. (1990a). Bridge, drawbridge, sandbar or island. In L. Albrecht & R. M. Brewer (Eds.). *Bridges of power: Women's multicultural alliances* (pp. 216-231). Santa Cruz, CA: New Society Publishers.

Anzaldua, G. (1990b). La conciencia de la mestiza: Towards a new consciousness. In G. Anzaldua (Ed.). *Making face, making soul/haciendo caras: Cre-*

ative and critical perspectives by women of color (pp. 377-389). San Francisco: Aunt Lute Foundation.

Bunch, C. (1978). Lesbian-Feminist Theory. In G. Vida (Ed.). *Our right to love: A lesbian resource book* (pp. 180-182). Englewood Cliffs, NJ: Prentice-Hall.

Butler, J. (1990). *Gender trouble: Feminism and the subversion of identity.* New York: Routledge.

Gaspar de Alba, A. (1993). Tortillerismo: Work by Chicana lesbians. *Signs: Journal of Women in Culture and Society, 18* (4), 956-963.

Hoagland, S. L. (1988). *Lesbian ethics: Toward new values.* Palo Alto, CA: Institute of Lesbian Studies.

Kanuha, V. (1990). Compounding the triple jeopardy: Battering in lesbian of color relationships. *Women & Therapy, 9*(1/2), 169-84.

Krestan, J. & Bepko, C. S. (1980). The problem of fusion in the lesbian relationship. *Family Process, 19,* 277-289.

Lorde, A. (1982). *Zami a new spelling of my name: A biomythography.* Freedom, CA: The Crossing Press.

Lorde, A. (1981). The master's tools will never dismantle the master's house. In C. Moraga & G. Anzaldua (Eds.). *This bridge called my back: Writings by radical women of color* (pp. 98-101). Watertown, MA: Persephone Press.

Lugones, M. (1990). Playfulness, "world" traveling, and loving perception. In G. Anzaldua (Ed.). *Making face, making soul/haciendo caras: Creative and critical perspectives by women of color* (pp. 390-402). San Francisco: Aunt Lute Foundation.

Minh-ha, T. T. (1990). Not you/like you: Post-Colonial women and the interlocking questions of identity and difference. In G. Anzaldua (Ed.). *Making face, making soul/haciendo caras: Creative and critical perspectives by women of color* (pp. 371-375). San Francisco: Aunt Lute Foundation.

Molina, P. (1990). Recognizing, accepting and celebrating our differences. In G. Anzaldua (Ed.). *Making face, making soul/haciendo caras: Creative and critical perspectives by women of color* (pp. 326-331). San Francisco: Aunt Lute Foundation.

Parker, P. (1990). For the white person who wants to know how to be my friend. In G. Anzaldua (Ed.). *Making face, making soul/haciendo caras: Creative and critical perspectives by women of color* (pp. 297-298). San Francisco: Aunt Lute Foundation.

Pederson, P. (1988). *A handbook for developing multicultural awareness.* Alexandria, VA.: American Association for Counseling and Development.

Rave, E. J. (1990). White Feminist therapists and anti-racism. *Women & Therapy, 9*(1/2), pp. 313-326.

Roberts, J. R. 1982. Black lesbians before 1970: A bibliographical essay. In M. Cruikshank (Ed.). *Lesbian studies: Present and future* (pp. 103-109). Old Westbury, NY: The Feminist Press.

Smith, B. (1983). *Home girls: A Black feminist anthology.* New York: Kitchen Table/Women of Color Press.

Solomon, B. B. (1976). *Black empowerment: Social work in oppressed communities.* New York: Columbia University Press.

Woodman. N. J. (1989). Mental health issues of relevance to lesbian women and gay men. *Journal of Gay & Lesbian Psychotherapy, 1*(1), 53-63.

Yamada, M. (1981). Asian Pacific American women and feminism. In C. Moraga & G. Anzaldua (Eds.). *This bridge called my back: Writings by radical women of color* (pp. 71-75). Watertown, MA: Persephone Press.

RESOURCE DIRECTORY OF ANTHOLOGIES BY WOMEN OF COLOR

Multicultural Anthologies

Anzaldua, G. (Ed.) (1990). *Making face, making soul/haciendo caras: Creative and critical perspectives by women of color.* San Francisco: Aunt Lute Foundation.

Lesbian Writing and Publishing Collective (Eds.) (1990). *Dykewords: An anthology of lesbian writing.* Toronto: Women's Press.

Moraga, C. & Anzaldua G. (Eds.) (1981). *This bridge called my back: Writings by radical women of color.* Watertown, MA: Persephone Press.

Silverada, M. (Ed.) (1991). *Piece of my heart: A lesbian of color anthology.* Toronto: Sister Vision Woman of Color Press.

African American Anthologies

Brown, L. (1980). Dark horses: A view of writing and publishing by dark lesbians. *Sinister Wisdom, 13,* Spring, 45-50.

Hull, G. T., Scott, P. B. & Smith, B. (1982). *All the women are white, all the blacks are men, but some of us are brave.* Old Westbury, NY: Feminist Press.

Roberts, J. R. (Ed.) (1981). *Black lesbians: An annotated bibliography.* Florida: Naiad Press.

Shockley, A. A. (1979). The Black lesbian in American Literature: A critical overview. *Conditions: Five,* Autumn, 133-142.

Asian American Anthologies

Chung, C., Kim, A., Lemeshewsky, A. K. (Eds.) (1987). *Between the lines: An anthology.* Santa Cruz, CA: Dancing Bird.

Fernandez, S. et al. (Eds.) (1990). "Awakening Thunder: Asian Canadian Women," Special Issue of *Fireweed: A Feminist Quarterly,* no. 30.

Kobayashi, T. & Oikawa, M. (1993). *All names spoken.* Toronto: Sister Vision Woman of Color Press.

Lee, S. et al. (Eds.) (1990). *Telling it: Women and language across cultures.* Vancouver, B.C.: Press Gang.

Lim, S. G. et al. (Eds.) (1989). *The forbidden stitch: An Asian American women's anthology.* Corvallis, OR: Calyx Books.

Tsui, K. (1983). *The words of a woman who breathes fire.* San Francisco: Spinsters Ink.

Latina Anthologies

Ramos, J. (Ed.) (1987). *Compañeras: Latina lesbian: An anthology.* New York: Latina Herstory Project.

Trujillo, C. (Ed.) (1991). *Chicana lesbians: The girls our mothers warned us about.* Berkeley: Third Woman.

Native Anthologies

Brant, B. (Ed.) (1988). *A gathering of spirit: A collection by North American Indian women.* Ithaca, NY: Firebrand.

Roscoe, W. (Ed.) (1989). *Living the spirit: A gay American Indian anthology.* New York: St. Martin's.

The Norms of Conduct in Social Service Agencies: A Threat to the Mental Health of Puerto Rican Lesbians

Hilda Hidalgo

SUMMARY. The personal and professional situation of a Puerto Rican lesbian social worker is analyzed using feminist standpoint theory. Beginning within the circumstances of a specific group, this approach studies the effect of social structure on the lives of group members.

Social service agencies claim organizational policies protecting lesbians and gay men from workplace discrimination. However, these policies are rendered void by cultural norms of conduct in the workplace supporting de-facto discrimination. This pattern of discrimination adversely impacts the professional development of social workers, the quality of service to clients, and the overall mental health of both.

While some states have policies prohibiting employers and service providers from discriminating on the basis of sexual preference, most policies regulating employee benefits are based on mari-

---

Hilda Hidalgo, PhD, ACSW, is Professor Emerita at Rutgers, The State University of New Jersey, and Assistant Commissioner, Division of Professional Development and Licensing, New Jersey State Department of Education.

[Haworth co-indexing entry note]: "The Norms of Conduct in Social Service Agencies: A Threat to the Mental Health of Puerto Rican Lesbians." Hidalgo, Hilda. Co-published simultaneously in *Journal of Gay & Lesbian Social Services* (The Haworth Press, Inc.) Vol. 3, No. 2, 1995, pp. 23-41; and: *Lesbians of Color: Social and Human Services* (ed: Hilda Hidalgo) The Haworth Press, Inc., 1995, pp. 23-41; and: *Lesbians of Color: Social and Human Services* (ed: Hilda Hidalgo) Harrington Park Press, an imprint of The Haworth Press, Inc., 1995, pp. 23-41. Multiple copies of this article/chapter may be purchased from The Haworth Document Delivery Center [1-800-3-HAWORTH; 9:00 a.m. - 5:00 p.m. (EST)].

23

tal status and traditional family structure and thus do, in fact, discriminate against lesbians and gay men. In addition, most work environments, while not overtly hostile to gay and lesbian workers and clients are, nevertheless, "unfriendly" and oppressive since they follow the conduct norms of traditional organizational culture. The prevailing attitude in the workplace is similar to the newly-adopted military policy of "don't ask, don't tell." This "don't ask, don't tell" stance is based on the belief that sexual orientation should be kept private. This public/private dichotomy provides the socially-accepted rationalization that enables heterosexuals and "homophobes" to appear liberal or tolerant, while denouncing homosexual behaviors as unnatural or immoral.

The distinction between public and private spheres that "liberal" or "tolerant" policy makers impose on lesbians and gays is not imposed on heterosexuals. In fact, work environments publicly celebrate heterosexuality. Examples of such celebrations include: agency/organization-sponsored events and activities that recognize engagements, marriages, births and anniversaries; norms of conduct allowing employees to display photos of opposite-sex, significant others; and free discussion in collegiate conversations (at water fountain or in boardroom) of the joys and sorrows of heterosexual intimate relationships.

Many scholars and advocates for social justice have written about and documented the deceptiveness in the distinction between the public and private spheres (Bensimon, 1993; Ferguson, 1984; Harding, 1991; Martin, 1990).

The private/public dichotomy forces invisibility on a class of people earmarked for discrimination and oppression for being who they are. Minorities of color have a long history and experience in becoming "invisible" in order to escape their oppression. "Passing" was a strategy used by some Afro-Americans as a way to survive and advance in a racist society. Asians mutilated their faces to become more European in their appearance. Latinos worked hard at losing their accents and emphasizing their Spanish-European roots, minimizing their mestizo characteristics. All these strategies of "passing" extracted a heavy emotional price from those who viewed "passing" as their only option for acceptance, survival and socioeconomic advancement.

Studies conducted by several social work practitioners report that families of Puerto Rican lesbians generally use the public/private dichotomy as the focus of advice on workplace conduct given to relatives who "come out" to them (Arroyo et al., 1986; Hidalgo, 1984). Hidalgo, for example, reported that the Puerto Rican lesbians and gay men in her study identified employment discrimination as a major concern in obtaining and/or keeping their jobs/positions. A frequent statement by Puerto Rican lesbians in indepth interviews was, "I try to remain invisible–as far as being a lesbian; I am afraid that being "out" will jeopardize my employment–it is hard enough to be Puerto Rican and be employed/promoted; being lesbian and out at work is suicidal" (Hidalgo, 1984).

In line with the feminist tradition of critique, it can be demonstrated that (1) the public/private dichotomy obscures and perpetuates inequities experienced by lesbians and gay men in their place of work, and (2) the lesbians of color are further affected by this dichotomy in their developmental journey to arrive at an "I am OK" perception of self.

To force or expect lesbians and gay men to separate the public and private spheres of their life is to overlook the "intimate relation" (Pateman, 1989) and dismiss concerns arising from a person's sexual orientation as private and separate from her/his other social roles (i.e., as a worker). Bensimon (1993) has observed that

> the logic that informs the public/private distinction to keep lesbians and gay men invisible in the work place is partial, distorting and perverse. It is *partial* because it is derived from a vision of the public that takes into account only the reality of the dominant heterosexual class. It is *distorting* because it normalizes sexuality as heterosexuality. It is *perverse,* because it provides justification to continue the oppression of lesbians and gays in the work place and in society.

The intent of this paper is to show concretely that accepting the logic behind the public/private dichotomy represents a "mental health hazard" to lesbians and gay men. This hazard has a compounding detrimental effect on the lives of lesbians and gay men of color. To buy into the public/private dichotomy is to adopt a practice that prevents liberation and self actualization . . . a practice that is personally and socially stultifying to homosexuals and heterosexuals alike.

To focus and clarify the dangers inherent in acceptance of the public/private dichotomy, I apply knowledge grounded in the "life story" (Denzen, 1989; Titon, 1980) of "Maria," a social worker, who self-identifies as a lesbian.

My approach builds on the work done by Estela Bensimon (in which she effectively argues the fallacy and perversity of the private/public dichotomy) in relation to gays and lesbians in the institutions of higher education (Bensimon, 1993).

Maria was interviewed in the summer of 1993, and her story serves to illustrate how the public/private dichotomy stagnates the developmental process of lesbians of color toward a positive self-image and contributes to the invisibility of lesbians in community leadership roles that many Puerto Rican lesbians have played.

Since this paper focuses exclusively on Maria's story, it describes a Puerto Rican lesbian's existence and should not be assumed to encompass the experience of Puerto Rican gay men. There are significant differences in the experiences and "standpoints" of lesbians and gay men as the result of the socialization process of men and women in the Puerto Rican society.[1]

I have relied on *feminist standpoint epistemology* (Harding, 1986; 1991; Hartsock, 1983) for interpreting Maria's life experience so as to demonstrate specific ways in which the public/private dichotomy contributes to the erosion of developmental processes and prevents, for lesbians of color, the integration of self-respect attributes into an "I am OK" wholeness.

Maria's life story provides a feminist-lesbian standpoint from which to view the effects which the public/private logic has on her as a *social worker in a multi-service family agency.* I am aware that Maria's interpretation of her own situation as well as any interpretation of Maria are shaped by individual circumstances and circumstances that are particular to the social service agency where she practices. I am not suggesting that her experience can be generalized to all social service agencies nor that her life provides a complete view of social service agencies from the perspective of Latina human service providers. Rather, by means of Maria's story, I provide a view of human service agencies that for the most part has been repressed, at least within the body of literature that addresses concerns of lesbians of color, especially Puerto Ricans. Studies have not considered how human service agencies, as patriarchal institutions, with an ingrained heterosexual ideology and cultural norms, create a set of circumstances that in effect assume control over the "private" life of lesbians, and lead them to experience "public" life as employees in ways that are unimaginable to those who are the beneficiaries of the privileges of heterosexuality and eurocentric status.

The silence around lesbian and gay concerns in the social service literature could be attributed to the fact that professional organizations and researchers were primarily concerned with addressing discrimination based on race and gender. Many of the most respected leaders in the human service professions, including some lesbian and gay Afro-Americans and Puerto Ricans, argue that documenting subjective experiences of gays and lesbians for inclusion in the record of discriminatory practices will lead to fragmentation and divisiveness, and will be counterproductive to the primary goal: to end discrimination based on race/gender. On a more personal and political level, it may also be said that the societal taboos and stigmas associated with homosexuality are strong deterrents to certain forms of research; for both straight and gay researchers to apply their expertise and skills to such inquiries is still perceived as detrimental to their professional careers.

A major obstacle in gaining access to study participants is the fear that "life stories" are more susceptible to providing clues that might reveal the identity of the subject. Maria, the woman on whose story I rely to challenge normative constructions of social service agencies, is very protective of her sexual identity and was quite ambivalent about her participation in this project. Even though she has been supportive of the project, she remains, even now, apprehensive about her role within it.

The next two sections describe the methodology used in this study:

1. The *"life story" framework* facilitates allowing a stranger (in this case a Puerto Rican lesbian) to add to our understanding of the detrimental effects of the public/private dichotomy on

the mental health of individuals burdened by multiple levels of oppression. "Life Story" provides a qualitative method of gathering and organizing data; and

2. *Feminist Standpoint Epistemology* provides an orientation and interpretive strategy for making sense of the interview material.

LIFE STORY AS A METHODOLOGICAL FRAMEWORK

In this paper I rely on life story methodology to present ways in which Maria manages the "public side" of her life at her agency. A life story consists of a "person-centered ethnography" through which researchers attempt "to portray lives of ordinary individuals, in cultures and contexts sometimes far removed from the ones they know, with the kind of perceptiveness and detail that transform a stranger we might meet in our personal lives into a friend" (Langness & Gelya, 1981, p. 1). Essentially, by presenting Maria's life story at a social service agency, I show a lesbian-structured reality that is often unknown to the majority of individuals who make up the agency's professional, paraprofessional and supportive staff.

Maria's life story at her social work agency was primarily reconstructed from an initial two-and-a-half hour interview and several follow-up conversations directed toward clarifying those passages on which I rely to make the point that the public/private dichotomy, since it prevents personal liberation and self-actualization, represents a mental health hazard in the lives of lesbians of color.

The initial interview was conducted in Maria's home, where she would feel more comfortable in telling her story. She was aware that the interviewer was a Puerto Rican social worker, a lesbian who works as a top level administrator in an educational-focused institution.

Maria read her story as recorded by the interviewer and reacted as to the extent to which it captures her feelings, thoughts and interpretations.

To make sense of Maria's story I adopted a methodological convention inspired by Denzen's (1989) methods of interpretive biography. I provide Maria's own words, a short segment of her life story at her social service agency and then turn to feminist standpoint theory as an interpretive strategy to anchor the meaning of this life story segment within the larger cultural context of a large multi-service agency.

Feminist Standpoint Epistemology as Interpretive Strategy

The "public/private" distinction in most organizations/agencies universalizes sexuality as *heterosexuality,* blinding those who belong to the dominant sexual class (both women and men) to the very specific ways in which they impose invisible and intolerable existences on lesbian staff. The invisibility of lesbian staff within the agency is maintained by their public/private distinction. To understand the meaning of such an invisible existence requires an epistemology that is centered on the situation of the lesbian staff member. It calls for an epistemology that is grounded in *her* interpretation and understanding of the public sphere . . . a sphere that the institutional culture limits to "heterosexuals only."

Standpoint theory can help to eliminate areas of ignorance: "starting thought from the (many different) daily activities of lesbians it enables us to see things that might otherwise have been invisible to us, not just about those lives but about heterosexual women's lives and men's lives, straight as well as gay" (Harding, 1991).

Using lesbian standpoint, we must reject the notion that the experience of women is universal regardless of sexual orientation, race and social class. Viewing the public sphere of social service agencies through the eyes of those who are in the margins changes the one-dimensional and incomplete vision and stimulates a different, more complete understanding of the "center's" own situation as well as of the situation they create for others (Harding, 1991).

A Puerto Rican lesbian standpoint has the valuable capacity of revealing how the vision of the dominant heterosexual, white and eurocentric class structures in the public sphere can be oppressive and threatening to lesbians of color who must constantly struggle to construct their lives within it. It helps us see how that structure has an adverse effect on the developmental journey of Puerto Rican lesbians working to achieve an "OK" vision of themselves.

Feminist standpoint epistemology provides a framework from which Puerto Rican lesbian-centered reality clashes with the "norm" of patriarchal heterosexual construction of the workplace. This epistemology urges us to "walk in the other person's shoes" rather than making her/him an appendix of preexisting dominant frameworks.

Feminist standpoint theories reject "the notion of an 'unmediated truth', arguing that knowledge is mediated by a host of factors related to an individual's particular position in a determinate sociopolitical formation at a specific point in history" (Hawkesworth, 1990). Accordingly, in this paper, the way Maria experiences the social service agency in which she works provides the knowledge for a reality that is oppositional to the taken-for-granted reality of the dominant sexual class. The intent is not merely to describe Maria's experiences but also to describe the reality of her workplace as viewed from her particular situation, which is different from the view of heterosexual workers.

LESBIAN EXISTENCE AT "LA FAMILIA" MULTISERVICE AGENCY: A DIFFERENT AND UNEXAMINED EXPERIENCE

"La Familia," where Maria holds a position as a supervisor of a social service unit, is a state-supported agency that provides a variety of services to low-income families in a large city. Maria holds an MSW degree and started as a caseworker in "La Familia" with a BA degree 10 years ago. Three years ago she was promoted to supervisor and has a total of 15 social workers under her supervision. La Familia is a state agency and persons holding social worker positions do not necessarily hold a BSW or MSW degree, although a Bachelors degree is required. Maria is the highest ranking "Hispanic" professional in her agency. (The Hispanic label is used by the agency for the "equal opportunity employers'" statistical reports.) As an MSW, Maria is aware of the National Association of Social Workers' (NASW) policy in regard to lesbian and gay issues (NASW Delegate Assembly 1993), but was not aware of the Council on Social Work Education's (CSWE) policy of mandating inclusion of gay and lesbian issues in the curriculum; she stated, however, that in her MSW program lesbian and gay issues were addressed from a nonheterosexist perspective. She identified her MSW experience as helpful in dealing with some of her internalized heterosexism and homophobia.

Maria characterized the climate of her workplace as patriarchal and homophobic/heterosexist. Her supervisor is a married male and Maria does not know any person at or above her own rank in the agency who is gay/lesbian. She knows a professional worker in another unit who is gay and a secretary who is a lesbian. Maria is in the closet and lives full of "secret fears" of being "outed" and of "coming out" to her colleagues, superiors and subordinates. In her interview she cited examples of remarks and jokes made by employees that were derogatory toward gays and lesbians and that were echoed/applauded by other staff present.

Maria's performance evaluations rate her as "exceptional" in all categories and she is frequently praised by her supervisor for what he evaluates as "consistent, excellent in the discharge of her duties" and as "always willing to go beyond the call of duty." She is recommended for a promotion as soon as the salary/promotion freeze in the agency is lifted. As I show in the sections that follow, Maria feels stressful demands, as a Puerto Rican lesbian "who made it," to perform carefully orchestrated acts of "closetedness" (Sedgwick, 1990).

Managing the Public by Hiding the Private

In an agency where heterosexuality is the norm and sexuality and sexual identity are viewed as private and personal concerns that are separate from the public act of being a staff member, there are compelling, if not coercive, reasons for Maria to remain silent about being a lesbian. To explain how she meets the demands that arise from the assumption of universal heterosexuality, she says, "I try to look very feminine, I seldom wear any pantsuits although pantsuits are accepted and appropriate professional attire for women, and other married and single women do wear them to work." When asked by the interviewer if she thinks that all the staff would react negatively to her if she "comes out," and if she did not think the Governor's order to prohibit discrimination in state agencies on the basis of sexual orientation would protect her, Maria replied,

> while some people who like me and are close to me might accept me and keep treating me the same way they did when they did not know I was a lesbian, I think the majority will

react negatively. They might not say anything in front of me but in subtle ways they will use it against me. Maybe I am a little paranoid but it took me a long time to get where I am. I was the first Puerto Rican in my unit, and the first to be promoted to a supervisor's position. I have received a lot of rejection from teachers in school and from society in general for being Latina and I have learned to live and cope with it. Enough is enough!

I have worked hard to be accepted by the staff and I don't want to spoil that now by "coming out." While the state bureaucracy is large, I work in a smaller field unit and with people constantly being moved from one unit location to another the word gets around. I have been in government service long enough to know that affirmative action and anti-discrimination policies do not protect people. There is a way to get around them. They might not say it is because you are Puerto Rican or a lesbian that you are not getting promoted or hired, but you know that it is a major part of it. You think I am paranoid? I am not; it is a reality. I am at the top of the civil service list for the next promotion and I am not going to let my "private business" interfere in my professional life.

Maria's statements exemplify the interlocking nature of oppression (Collins, 1986) and the struggle for survival. As a Puerto Rican, a woman and a lesbian in an institution that is male and heterosexually-dominated, Maria is subject to simultaneous sources of oppression that regulate her conduct in the public sphere of the social service agency. To avoid compromising her career and being deprived of relationships with her coworkers, Maria constructs her life according to the prescribed script of assumed heterosexuality.

Maria has *internalized* the private/public distinction; thus, she cooperates with the dominant heterosexist work culture which wants to keep her invisible. The norms and culture of the workplace are more powerful than the Governor's executive order that prohibits discrimination based on gender, national origin, race and sexual orientation. The majority of workers in the agency have not lived an experience that mirrors Maria's. As a matter of fact, they are constantly bringing their heterosexual private experiences to their public life and the agency celebrates and recognizes their marriages, the birth of their children, their dates, and in some instances their heterosexual extramarital affairs.

It is this very *partiality* in experience that makes the public/private dichotomy a distinction that *distorts reality;* for it fails to see that in the public space those essential freedoms–and I am thinking here in particular of the freedom to interact in the public space without having to hide one's sexual orientation–are systematically granted to the heterosexual staff and are withheld from "others." In order to survive–not to risk her career, not to be isolated, not to be rejected, not to be seen as abnormal–Maria is conscious, always, of being assessed from and by the vantage point of heterosexuality. She does not have the same freedom to interact in the public space that heterosexual people have; to avoid calling attention to herself she has to produce a "Maria" that does not challenge the heterosexual script of "normal" sexual relations, nor the male script of what a woman should be like.

Public Dominance of the Private

Maria lives in a small suburban town in the southern part of New Jersey, a community in the heart of the rural agricultural area of the state. The larger community surrounding the agency is conservative. It consists predominantly of heterosexual traditional anglo families, with a nearby area that has a concentration of Latinos, many of whom work as migrant agricultural workers.

The isolated and conservative locale of La Familia agency and Maria's place of residence (where the closest city is several hours away) creates a kind of institutional closure that "brings into play a particular, and sometimes very powerful set of organizational controls over time and space, over sexual time and sexual bodies" (Hearn et al., 1989). The geographical location tightens its grip over the private lives of lesbians, for inside and outside the walls of La Familia Agency there are no "clear sexual zoning, territories that are gay and lesbian" (Hearn, 1989).

In the initial interview Maria was asked if she participated in the activities of the New Jersey NASW Chapter on Gay and Lesbian issues. Her response was:

No, I am afraid that someone will see me and the word will get out. I have been tempted to go to the lesbian and gay presentations that have been part of other professional conferences I have attended, such as the conference for AIDS service providers and other NASW sponsored conferences; but I have always attended [the conferences] with other members of the agency staff and everyone knows which sessions everyone is attending. I will have to get my supervisor's approval and this will be equivalent to "coming out" to him, something I don't want to do.

Whether or not her supervisor will be receptive to approval of Maria's attendance at professional conferences dealing with gay and lesbian issues is a moot point; Maria responds to her own sensed repression and curtails her interactions in public so that she can "pass." Unlike her colleagues who are free to choose the conferences and sessions in conferences that interest them and that contribute to their professional development, Maria is shackled by her own internalization of what would be valued in the area of professional development.

Constructing Public Interactions as a Lesbian Social Worker

The public/private dichotomy is further distorting because it reduces lesbianism to sexuality. The logic of the public/private is grounded in the belief that being lesbian is merely an issue of what one chooses to do in private and with whom. But this view is distorting for it is based on a logic that fails to hear and see what is so obvious and natural for Maria. She says, "My life as a Puerto Rican lesbian affects my view of the world."

For Maria being lesbian, as being a woman, translates into a particular construction of public life as a member of a professional family that impacts her social relations. This was clearly illustrated in her comments about her participation at professional conferences. She deprives herself of participating in professional development activities that might impact favorably on her professional performance. Maria's invisibility as a lesbian prevents her from expanding her professional network and making "public contact" with other lesbians and gay social workers and human service professionals . . . contact that could benefit both clients and herself.

Private Lives and Public Policies

As long as sexual orientation is a private matter, the policies that benefit employees in recognized legal heterosexual relationships will continue to be denied to lesbian and gay employees. In Maria's story, she and her partner share their financial resources. Maria's partner is self-employed and has to pay as an individual for health insurance. If Maria could include her life partner in the state health benefits package, as married couples can, it would represent a savings of over two thousand dollars a year in cost plus many additional services that her life partner does not receive from her individual health insurance package. Maria would very much like to see personnel policies that recognize her relationship, but she is not willing to become visible and join in the open struggle of lesbians and gay activists to change discriminatory practices against lesbians and gays in the workplace and in the law.

She expresses psychological pain in what she calls "her cowardliness of not speaking out to end injustices perpetuated against lesbians and gays." This is especially painful for her since she has actively participated in and led public struggles to end discrimination based on ethnicity and race. She feels a sense of disloyalty to herself and a sense of duplicity and inconsistency in what she views as her obligation to oppressed people. (This is especially so since she has, based on her education and employment, a rather privileged place in society.) In this regard she is in constant struggle between what she believes is morally correct (combat injustice) and the "self serving" closeted posture that protects her from abuse and discrimination.

A New View of the Workplace

The dominant view of the public is based on knowledge derived from the lives of men in the dominant races, classes, and cultures (Harding, 1991), and therefore obscures the inequalities that arise within the public space for the Puerto Rican social work employee who is a lesbian and a member of the "second sex." The public/private logic is persuasive and it has been used effectively to maintain lesbian and gay persons "in the closet."

Maria's narrative shows that the public space of La Familia Social Agency, in being structured by the prevailing assumption of heterosexuality, forces her into a pattern of living and relating to others that is centered on hiding, on remaining invisible, on feeling conflicted and "incomplete."

Because Maria's story emerges from someone who occupies the "borderline" position (Anzaldua, 1987) of "stranger" or "outsider within," it brings into the open aspects of life in the workplace that have been left out of normative constructions of the social work profession and the agencies that deliver social services. Her account is particularly revealing in that it magnifies the ways institutionalized heterosexism, homophobia and ethnocentrism force Maria to be silent, not voicing felt inequalities for fear of even greater rejection and marginalization. Maria's account shows that what is assumed to be normal–a public space that is structured exclusively according to the norms of heterosexuality–is in fact *abnormal* in that it forces her and others like her into unnatural lives in order to survive.

When we look at the institution of compulsory heterosexuality from Maria's vantage point, it is possible to see the irrationalities it produces: a life of dissimulation so as not to breach the distinctions between the public and private; a fear of rejection; and a concerted effort to erase from her social work practice issues having to do with sexual orientation, even though these issues may be highly relevant to her work and to the clients the agency serves. The vision of the workplace that emerges from Maria's life is very different from the vision of heterosexual workers who would have us believe that sexual orientation is a private and personal matter, separate from the public space and therefore irrelevant. Maria's story challenges normative constructions of professional life in human service agencies. We need to grasp and examine the view that emerges from Maria's account of her experience within a public space that sees her as an anomaly. Examination of this view provides a distinctive analysis and interpretation that is not presently available in conventional discourses related to participation in personnel policies, employee benefits packages, and professional/human development on the job.

The Separation of Public and Private:
A Detriment to Mental Health

Mental health is defined as a relative state of emotional well-being, freedom from incapacitating conflicts, and the consistent ability to make and carry out our rational decisions and cope with environmental stresses and internal pressures (Barker, 1987).

The public/private distinction is detrimental to mental health to the degree that it forces an individual to spend most of her working day in conflict, avoiding words and actions that might expose to others who she really is. The private/public distinction creates additional economic burdens, adding to stress and generating powerful internal pressures as the individual copes with repressed anger, feelings of dishonesty, and is disempowered from making decisions in her best interest. Maria's psychological defense of "passing" erodes her self-respect and therefore makes her feel that she is a "not OK" person.

She might argue that her closetedness constitutes a source of resistance, a personal and private resistance and a refusal to be further victimized (Hoagland, 1988). Maria's silence prevents her from falling into what Barry (1979) conceives as "victimism." She creates a framework for others to know her as a successful Puerto Rican professional while denying her total humanity and her whole experience–denying heterosexuals the privilege of abusing her.

CONCLUSION: ARGUMENTS FOR A NEW STANDPOINT

Nancy Hartsock advocates for the feminist standpoint by pointing out that "women's lives make available a particular and privileged vantage point on male supremacy, a vantage point that can ground a powerful critique of the phallocractic institutions and ideology that constitute the capitalist form of patriarchy" (1983, p. 231). In a similar manner, it may be said that Maria's life story as a Puerto Rican lesbian social worker also provides a particular and privileged vantage point that can ground a powerful critique of the oppressiveness of institutionalized heterosexual norms within the workplace.

Maria's view of the agency, though partial and incomplete, provides knowledge and insight that can move us toward the development of a *lesbian standpoint* from which to view and interpret social service institutions. This paper provides several compelling reasons for creating and using such a standpoint:

1. Recognizing the danger of damaging internalized norms. The knowledge derived from Maria's life takes us to a different level of understanding of the myriad ways in which the institution of compulsory heterosexuality controls the lives of lesbian workers. In particular, looking at the social service agency through her eyes makes us aware that although the vision of the work climate produced by the public/private dichotomy is partial, distorting, and perverse it cannot be dismissed simply as being false (Hartsock, 1983), for it is a vision that comes true as long as it forces Maria to structure her life in accordance with heterosexual norms and expectations. Maria's constant vigilance against departure from the prescribed script of heterosexuality reveals how very powerful and controlling this vision can be and how it erodes self-confidence and negatively affects the mental health of the individual.

2. Ensuring the visibility and freedom of all women. Accounts like Maria's uncover repressed stories which help us develop a new and different analysis of the workplace and life within social service agencies. A lesbian standpoint enables us to see that, just as Maria's existence as a social worker/supervisor is controlled by structures that render her particular being and reality invisible, all women in the social welfare structure struggle to fit in, to become part of the structures that are defined by knowledge derived from the experience of the heterosexual eurocentric male.

Maria's story, then, acquires a broader value, for women's reality has been always viewed as private and confined to "her home." That privacy, in fact, serves the interest of ensuring the continuing oppression of women.

3. Examining heterosexual privilege. A lesbian standpoint magnifies and, therefore, brings into sharp relief heterosexual privilege. It provokes an awareness of how privilege is derived from one's sexual orientation, a privilege which from "the perspective of heterosexual women's lives . . . appears simply as 'the way things are,' perhaps as part of nature" (Harding, 1991, p. 258).

Such a standpoint exposes the compromises, premeditated actions, and the performances of closetedness that the institution of compulsory heterosexuality forces on lesbians (and gay men); it also awakens consciousness about our own and others' unexamined privileges. It makes us ask in what ways the system that induces Maria to dissimulate who she is so as to "avoid negative relationships with her colleagues" and makes her fearful "of being rejected at the human level" might force others (for example, heterosexual women) to also remain silent about the myriad ways in which the public discourse subjects them to sexism, lest they call attention to their own "anomaly" and are discounted even further.

4. Building for human empowerment, self-realization and health. A lesbian standpoint can be humanizing and transformative. Maria's story provides a strong directive to take into account that workers' lives are shaped not only by the content of their labor but also by the context within which their labor is carried out. Her story makes it less possible for us to see life in the workplace "from a perspective of unexamined heterocentricity" (Rich, 1986a, p. 24).

A lesbian standpoint can serve as a catalyst for workplace changes designed to lessen the stresses which impair workers' mental health. It can help us see and remove institutional barriers which render people fearful, silent and disempowered, and which prevent both clients and service providers from reaching full productivity and self-realization.

NOTE

1. Most social science research–including studies on homosexuality–has been based on male examples. "Lesbians have historically been deprived of a political existence through inclusion as female versions of male homosexuality. To equate lesbian existence with male homosexuality because each is stigmatized is to erase female reality once again" (Rich, 1980). The "invisibility" generally experienced by lesbians in being subsumed in male homosexuality is even further compounded for lesbians of color.

REFERENCES

Anzaldua, G. (1987). *Borderlands: The new Mestiza/la frontera.* San Francisco, California: Spinsters/Aunt Lute Book Company,

Arroyo, D., Arroyo, G., Olan, C. L. & Sanchez-Soto, H. (1986). Puerto Rican lesbians and the "coming out" process. Unpublished Master's Thesis, Rutgers University School of Social Work, New Jersey.

Barker, R. L. (1987). *The social work dictionary.* Silver Springs, Maryland: National Association of Social Workers.

Barry, K. (1979). *Female sexual slavery.* Englewood Cliffs, New Jersey: Prentice-Hall.

Bensimon, E. M. (1993). Lesbian existence and the challenge to normative construction of the academy. *Journal of Boston University, 174*(3), 199-202.

Collins, P. H. (1986). Learning from the outsider within: The sociological significance of Black feminist thought. *Social Problems, 33*(6), 14-32.

Denzen, N. K. (1989). *Interpretive biography.* Newbury Park, California: Sage Publications.

Ferguson, K. E. (1984). *The feminist case against bureaucracy.* Philadelphia: Temple University Press.

Greene, M. (1988). *The dialectic of freedom.* New York: Teachers College Press.

Harding, S. (1986). *The science question in feminism.* Ithaca, New York: Cornell University Press.

Harding, S. (1991). *Whose science? Whose knowledge?: Thinking from women's lives.* Ithaca, New York: Cornell University Press.

Hartsock, N. C. M. (1983). *Money, sex, and power: Toward a feminist historical materialism.* Boston: Northeastern University Press.

Hawkesworth, M. E. (1990). *Beyond oppression: Feminist theory and political strategy.* New York: The Continuum Publishing Company.

Hearn, J., Sheppard, D. L., Tancred-Sheriff, P. & Burrell, G. (1989). *The sexuality of organization.* Beverly Hills, California: Sage Publications.

Hidalgo, H. (1984). The Puerto Rican lesbian in the United States. In T. Darty & S. Potter (Eds.). *Women-Identified women* (pp. 105-115). Palo Alto, California: Mayfield Publishing Company.

Hoagland, S. L. (1988). *Lesbian ethics: Toward new value.* Palo Alto, California: Institute of Lesbian Studies.

Kitzinger, C. (1990). Beyond the boundaries: Lesbians in academe. In S. Stiver-Lie & V. O'Leary (Eds.). *Storming the tower: Women in the academic world* (pp. 28-39). London: Nicholas Publishing.

Kitzinger, C. (1987). *The social construction of lesbianism.* Beverly Hills, California: Sage Publications.

Langness, L. L. & Gelya, F. (1981). *Lives: An anthropological approach to biography.* Novato, California: Chandler & Sharp Publishers.

MacKinnon, C. A. (1989). *Toward a feminist theory of the state.* Cambridge, Massachusetts: Harvard University Press.

Martin, J. (1990). Deconstructing organizational taboos: The suppression of gender conflict in organizations. *Academy of Management Review, 15*, 339-357.

National Association of Social Workers (1993). Code of Ethics. Silver Spring, Maryland: NASW.

National Association of Social Workers (1980). NASW Policy Statements, NASW Delegate Assembly. Silver Spring, Maryland: NASW.

Pateman, C. (1989). *The disorder of women: Democracy, feminism and political theory.* Stanford, California: Stanford University Press.

Rich, A. (1986a). Compulsory heterosexuality. In A. Rich (Ed.). *Blood, bread, and poetry: Selected prose 1979-1985* (pp. 23-76). New York: W. W. Norton.

Rich, A. (1986b). Invisibility in Academe. In A. Rich. *Blood, bread, and poetry: Selected prose 1979-1985* (pp. 198-202). New York: W. W. Norton.

Sedwick, E. K. (1990). *Epistemology of the closet.* Berkeley, California: University of California Press.

Tierney, W. G. (1991). Public roles, private lives: Gay faculty in academe (unpublished paper).

Titon, J. T. (1980). The life story. *Journal of American Folklore, 93*, 276-292.

Whose Daughter Are You?
Exploring Identity Issues
of Lesbians Who Are Adopted

Mi Ok Bruining

SUMMARY. Lesbian women who are adopted confront a unique set of challenges including coming out, searching or not searching for birth families, and managing relationships with adoptive and birth families (if they are found). This article explores how adopted lesbians negotiate these issues, and how such issues impact the dual yet separate elements which contribute to identity: being adopted and being lesbian. The findings of a study of self-identified lesbians who are adopted are discussed. One of the central findings is that the women interviewed for this study were more comfortable with their lesbian identity than with their adoptive identity.

Lesbian women who are adopted are often confronted with a unique set of challenges in their process of developing a secure sense of identity. They must face a variety of issues, including negotiating the coming-out process, managing relationships with both adoptive and birth families (if they have found their birth parent(s)), and searching or not searching for their birth family. Exploring how adopted lesbians negotiate these issues is the pur-

Mi Ok Bruining, MSW, is a Social Worker, Social Work and Discharge Planning Department, Beth Israel Medical Center, New York, NY.

[Haworth co-indexing entry note]: "Whose Daughter Are You? Exploring Identity Issues of Lesbians Who Are Adopted." Bruining, Mi Ok. Co-published simultaneously in *Journal of Gay & Lesbian Social Services* (The Haworth Press, Inc.) Vol. 3, No. 2, 1995, pp. 43-60; and: *Lesbians of Color: Social and Human Services* (ed: Hilda Hidalgo) The Haworth Press, Inc., 1995, pp. 43-60; and: *Lesbians of Color: Social and Human Services* (ed: Hilda Hidalgo) Harrington Park Press, an imprint of The Haworth Press, Inc., 1995, pp. 43-60. Multiple copies of this article/chapter may be purchased from The Haworth Document Delivery Center [1-800-3-HAWORTH; 9:00 a.m. - 5:00 p.m. (EST)].

43

pose of this paper. It examines the dual yet separate elements which contribute to an identity: being adopted and being a lesbian. There has been a paucity of research on the process of identity formation of adopted lesbians. This paper makes an initial step in addressing this need by reporting the results of an interview study of 13 adopted lesbians.

The identity issues adopted lesbians face are summarized in three questions: Where did I come from? Who am I now? Where am I going? These questions are more difficult to answer when the context of family, genealogical, cultural and social histories have been disrupted—as in adoption.

Identity formation is the process of developing an individual's being and sense of self. In the study of personality the term "identity" can be defined as the essence and continuity of a person's self where the concept of oneself is internalized and subjective (Reber, 1985).

Recent studies and research focus on female identity development as having moral distinctions and intrapsychic differences from male identity development (Gilligan, 1982). Current theoretical debates challenge the theory that female development is similar to male development. Both contemporary and/or feminist academic and clinical perspectives challenge the historically white, male-dominated and partriarchally-defined content of theory about female identity. Current research suggests, for example, that female identity formation does not depend predominantly upon the achievement of separation (as in male identity formation) but is defined through attachment (Gilligan, 1982).

This paper explores the issues of women who are self-identified lesbians, that is, women who have "come out" as lesbians themselves and/or to others.

In Chapman and Brannock's (1987) article on lesbian identity development, it is argued that homosexual feelings in women originate from identification with (and possibly sexual transference towards) the mother. As a result of these early identifications with the mother, homosexual feelings may consciously and actively be accessible in all women's lives.

In her article on internalized homophobia and lesbian identity, Sophie (1987) presents her theory of lesbian identity in a linear fashion–these women "come out" in a series of identifiable stages, within the context of and as a reaction to homophobia. Recently, Sophie's theory of the development of lesbian identity has been challenged. MacCowan (1987) emphasizes that lesbian identity can also reflect a political response to sexism and oppression. She argues that lesbian identity also can reflect more of a political identity and less of a sexual behavior.

The adult adopted population is a particular group that has not been visible in the lesbian community. Lesbians also have not been visible in the "adoption community" of adopted persons, birth parents and adoptive parents, which make up the adoption triad. Recently, adopted lesbians have mobilized to address their unique issues (Baer, 1990-1991). These efforts have been concentrated on the West and East coasts of the U.S.A. For the majority of adopted lesbians, structured clinical, social, and political support systems are virtually nonexistent. The "Chain of Life" is the only published newsletter that focuses on adoption-related issues from a feminist perspective, including adopted lesbians (Baer, 1990).

Researchers have begun to study the ramifications of separation, loss, grief and anger in adopted individuals and the effect of adoption upon this development of identity (Deeg, 1991).

Being both adopted and a lesbian are identities which have been historically shame-based and stigmatized in one's own family system, as well as in society. Thus, in the context of homophobia and historical social stigma, adoption issues can be more complicated when the adopted person is a lesbian. These potential challenges, which combined adopted and lesbian issues, have not yet been documented in the social work literature.

Adoption is an enduring social phenomenon which has undergone many transitions in society. The definition of adoption is "to take (a child of other parents) as one's own child" (Woolf, 1972). Some form of adoption has been widely implemented for thousands of years in almost every culture.

Laws were created to protect the rights of children and parents when children were designated as the property of a family (Lifton, 1988). These laws instituted adoption as the formal transferral of these rights from one set of parents (birth parents) to another set of parents (adoptive parents), usually when the birth parents were dead or unable to properly take care of the children. In the circumstances of living birth parents, the practice of relinquishment was developed to legally convey their parenthood rights to the adoptive parents (Chesler, 1988).

In Western European countries and in the U.S.A., such adoptions were "closed." All identifying information and documents were protected and sealed within the locked files of adoption agencies. Until recently, to be adopted was to be "closeted" (Lifton, 1988). In the 1960s when the political and social climates of society were changing, adoption was still a secret, a taboo, a stigma, and a silence (Lifton, 1988).

Open adoptions are a recent phenomenon, in part a response to the increasing number of adopted adults who, in their search for information on their birth parents, were challenging the practice of closed adoptions (Caplan, 1990).

In 1950, adoption practice changed from being a predominantly intra-cultural/racial phenomenon to a practice that included cross-cultural/racial adoptions, as well as special needs children (older, physically disabled, mildly mentally retarded, etc.). However, most adoption agencies did not implement cross-cultural *education* for social workers or adoptive families until after there were disruptions in the adoptive families. A few post-adoption services have also been created to address the possibility of cross-cultural issues for these adoptive families (Bruining, 1990).

The Association of Black Social Workers (ABSW) has declared that adoption placements of African American children into white families perpetuates cultural genocide (Gilman, 1977). A large population of Native Americans agree with the ABSW's statement that cross-cultural adoption of children of color into Anglo families is cultural genocide (Kim, 1978). Andujo (1988), in researching Hispanic adoptees, supports the concept that cultural genocide can result from transethnic adoption. Her study found, for example, that transethnic adopted Hispanic children identified themselves as Americans (non-Hispanics). All of the same-ethnic Hispanic adopted children strongly identified themselves as Hispanic.

The term "adopted child" has historically been made in reference to adopted individuals. Even individuals who are adults are referred to as "adopted children" in the adoption community and within the adoption triad. This term may contribute to the pervasive attempts and efforts for empowerment to adopted people. Some adopted persons reject this term for these reasons (Lifton, 1988). As adults, many adopted people are reclaiming their own identities in an attempt to become more visible and to dismantle their feelings of powerlessness within the adoption community, the triad, and society in general.

"Searching" is viewed by many adult adopted persons as a vital element in the development or completion of their identity as whole, complete persons (Sachdev, 1991). "Searching" is also part of adopted persons' journey toward acceptance of the circumstances of their lives (Rosenweig-Smith, 1987). "Searching" by adopted persons can be considered a betrayal of loyalty towards the adoptive parents and birth parents (Rosenweig-Smith, 1988).

Adopted persons' identity formation is a new area of study. Marquis and Detweiler (1985) identify several areas to explore: control, status, interpersonal outcomes, and self-descriptive characteristics. The self-descriptive characteristics generated by adopted persons in Marquis and Detweiler's study include: poor self-image, inferiority, insecurity, fearfulness, abnormality, and loneliness. Subjects reported powerlessness in directing their own lives; feeling like pawns who were used by the powerful. Adopted persons described feelings of isolation and difficulty in maintaining long-term relationships. They perpetually felt like outsiders, alienated from others, incomplete and false.

Sochoberg-Winterberg and Shannon's study (1988) compares the psychosocial adjustment of adopted adults with non-adopted adults. Non-adopted adolescents contend with separation issues, but adopted adolescents deal with both the symbolic loss as well as the actual loss of a previous set of parents (birth parents). This loss makes adolescent adopted persons more vulnerable to additional experiences of loss, rejection, or abandonment later in their development, eventually having significant impact upon their adulthood relationships (Sochoberg-Winterberg and Shannon, 1988). In an effort to resolve issues of loss, rejection, or abandonment, adult adopted persons often search for birth relatives (Kowal-Schilling, 1984). The repercussions of damaged identity reveal themselves in the difficulties these adopted adults had in the development and establishment of secure and stable relationships, the replication of rejection and abandonment experiences, and lack of trust and intimacy (Humphrey and Humphrey, 1989).

The author was not able to identify any published studies on adopted lesbians.

There is no singular lesbian identity or singular developmental theory of lesbian identity (Boston Lesbian Psychologies Collective [BLPC, 1987]). According to Sophie (1987), it can be concluded that positive lesbian identity is a significant developmental achievement involving one's own acceptance of sexual identity within the hostile environment of heterosexism, homophobia, and internalized heterosexism and homophobia by lesbians.

Recent literature views lesbian and gay identity development as a process of developing an awareness of one's concept of self (Stein and Cohen, 1986). Some recent studies have suggested that lesbian and gay identity formation occurs in five stages: sensitization, identity, confusion, identity assumption, and commitments (Troiden, 1989). These stages represent manifestations of the emotional, psychological, and developmental process which lesbians and gay men experience in their phases of "coming out" (Troiden, 1989). However, they do not necessarily reflect the steps for everyone's coming-out process.

Lukes and Land (1990) consider lesbians and gay men a sexual minority group with a unique culture. They assert that cultural identity is more than a situation of shared history, language, and tradition. It is a manifestation of self-conceptualization which is self-assigned or socially mandated. Adopting a cultural identity conceptualization of lesbian identity suggests an alternative conceptualization of the developmental stages of lesbian identity to the one presented by Troiden. Lukes and Land as well as MacCowan (1987) stress the importance of becoming involved in the lesbian identity formation.

The coming-out process has been found by Monteflores and Schultz (1978) to differ for lesbians and gay men. These writers note that both lesbians and gay men describe the coming-out process as including a transition from personal to public disclosure of same-sex attraction, the importance of initial involvement in lesbian or gay communities, socialization, fear of homophobia, and the pre-coming-out confusion as to whether or not "homosexuality" is a choice.

Homophobia and internalized homophobia are elements of the hostile environment within which lesbians (and gay men) come out, and which they experience throughout their lives. Margolies, Becker and Jackson-Brewer (1987) assert, for example, that "closeted" lesbians may experience more difficulty in their lives because they operate and function in a covert identity, having to deal with the constant fear of being discovered that they have been living a lie within their families, relationships, and workplaces. Their refusal to acknowledge their lesbianism may foster feelings of self-hatred and may impair the ability to trust, to relate with genuine emotions, and to gain a fulfilling sense of intimacy.

In summary, research and academic studies are lacking in regards to the identity formation of lesbians who are adopted. There are no data which discuss whether lesbians who are adopted experience similar or different processes of identity development from lesbians who are not adopted. There are also no data that explore the possible challenges to identity development among lesbians who are adopted.

This paper is an initial step in exploring issues on identity formation of lesbians who are adopted; it presents new data and information on lesbians who are adopted and can serve as a stepping stone for further research on this subject.

METHODOLOGY

This paper discusses an exploratory project designed to examine the identity development of lesbians who are adopted. The author reflected on experiences and stories reported by 13 adopted lesbians who agreed to be interviewed by the author. The sample included 11 Caucasians and 2 Women of Color from the New York/New Jersey area. The sample was self-selected and the participants did not know each other. The author placed advertisements requesting volunteers to be interviewed in two national publications–one a monthly, Boston-based feminist publication, the other a weekly, mainstream New York City-based newspaper. In addition, flyers were distributed to and posted in women's bookstores and to a few lesbian organizations.

In order to foster the most complete expression of personal reflection and feelings on issues of being lesbians and adopted, the interview focused on eliciting the particular standpoint of each respondent. The author used a set of questions to guide the process. Nine sections organized the interview guide: (1) personal information, (2) relationship status, (3) children/childhood, (4) counseling/therapy, (5) adoptive family, (6) adoption issues, (7) birth parents/family, (8) sexual identity/lesbian issues, and (9) personal conclusions and insights related to the topic of identity formation.

Interviews lasted an average of an hour and a half with each respondent. The subjects were often eloquent and elaborated on many of the questions. The author uses quotes throughout the paper to convey the standpoint of the respondents. The interviews were taped, affording the author the opportunity to listen to each interview several times in order to better capture the essence of the responses for her analysis.

The responses were categorized by themes, similarities and differences.

Demographic Summary

Thirteen (13) were interviewed for this study. Their ages ranged from 22 to 59 years old. Six of the women were between 21 and 30; five were between 30 and 40; and 2 were over 40 years old. The ethnic backgrounds of the respondents were as follows: eight were Anglo (white), three were Jewish, one was Asian-Pacific Islander, and one was Latina. All of the women participating in the study were college graduates. All of the women were employed. Ten of the women worked at professional jobs at the time of the study, and three had skilled technical jobs. All of the women lived within the northeast corridor (New York-Boston) of the United States. Eight of the women were in lesbian relationships at the time of the study. Only one woman had another adopted lesbian as a partner.

Relationships

All 13 women currently are or were involved in monogamous relationships. A lover of one of the subjects was also adopted. Only one subject had not discussed her adoption with her partner. Most women felt that their adoption was something to be shared with the woman they love because it is an integral part of who they are.

The character of the responses in this area is best expressed by one of the respondents:

> My adoption is an important factor of me. It is, of what I am about. It's very important that I discuss it with anyone and everyone. It's the foundation of me, basically, so I think it's important that I let anyone I'm dealing with know that I was adopted and (that) these were the circumstances. Basically, this is the foundation.

Children/Parenthood

Two women were mothers, one a birth mother, the other an adoptive mother. However, 11 respondents expressed interest in adopting children. In essence the respondents observed that being adopted persons made them more receptive and willing to adopt.

Therapy/Counseling

Only four women sought therapy related to lesbian or adoption issues. The majority noted that they had more difficulty dealing with their status as adopted persons than with their status as lesbians. For example, one woman described her adoption as a horrible experience. Her adopted family was a multiproblem family. This woman learned that she was adopted after she came out as a lesbian, and after her first therapeutic experience. The focus of the later therapeutic experience related mostly to issues about her adoption since she felt comfortable about being a lesbian.

Adoptive Parents/Family

Three of the subjects interviewed had no siblings. Of the remaining ten women, five had adopted siblings, and five had siblings who were born to their adoptive parents. One woman reported that her adopted brother was gay. One respondent was adopted by parents whose ethnic group was different than hers.

Adoption Issues

Women who were adopted as infants reported that they felt they were an integral part of the adopting family. Women adopted after they were six months old expressed confusion, and had questions regarding the time before they were adopted. Most women noted that they did not have much information about their birth parents, and that what limited information their adoptive parents did have was often shared with them. Most women emphasized the positive nature of their adoption stories. They affirmed their appreciation for being informed early in their lives that they were adopted.

Many of the women felt deep gratitude and obligation towards their adoptive parents. A few felt some guilt for their secret desires to search for information about their birth parents. That guilt often prevented many of them from "searching."

When asked about how their adoption affected them as adults, most of the women expressed feelings of loss for the birth mothers. One woman described her adoptive mother's response to the homosexuality of both of her adoptive children:

> This is very interesting. I'm a lesbian and out to my parents. My brother is also, he's gay (and adopted). And he came out to my parents later than I did. And his role in the family was the one good child and I was the bad child. So, it was scary to contemplate how my parents would feel, when number two child came out. So, it was really, touchy at one point with my mother. She's very traditional culturally, but she's not very religious. And she says, I think God has sent me my son and my daughter because if they had been in another family, being who they are–being a lesbian and a gay person–that God made this arrangement so they could be in a supportive family. I was very moved by that.

In responding to the same questions another subject stated:

> Well, not knowing how it feels not to be adopted, being adopted, I think I appreciate the pain my parents went through to adopt me. That was the choice that she didn't have to make.

That's a choice that you appreciate. You tend to want to do more for her.

When asked how each woman thought being adopted has affected her as an adult woman, most women spoke about issues of self-esteem, insecurity, fear of trust and intimacy, or feelings of inauthenticity. One respondent captured these sentiments in the following particularly poignant way:

> I don't know where I came from. Who are these people (birth parents)? Who do I look like? When you meet people with the same biological last name and you sit there and go, Do you look like me? I mean you get kind of paranoid and you watch shows on television and you sit there and you cry. And you don't know why you're crying. And you keep quiet, you don't want them (adoptive parents) to know you're crying about it, you keep it all inside. So it took a lot. Most of my traumatic things really do stem from being adopted and really not feeling like I belong anywhere and I think that it interfered with my relationships, also. I would go in and out of very bad relationships. I usually wound up with people who I thought needed me, so that means they would keep me. I just came to that conclusion. That was very difficult for me to see.

Searching

Only four of the thirteen women are currently or have searched for their birth parents/family. However, only two had found enough information to continue to pursue the search process. Eight women felt it was very important to have identifying information about birth parents/family made available to those adopted persons "searching." Reasons given by respondents who were not searching included the expense involved and that conditions in their lives constrained them from getting involved in what they perceived as a very time-consuming process.

Two women who were not searching were found by their birth mother and other birth relatives who were searching.

Birth Parents/Family

The two women who were found by their birth parents reported divergent experiences (one positive, one negative). The woman reporting the positive experience with her birth mother has remained in contact with her; while the woman reporting a negative experience has not sustained contact.

Adoptive and Sexual Identity Issues

The author's intent in asking questions around adoption and sexual identity was to explore the effects of adopting on the coming-out process.

Eleven women confirmed that their sexual identity and being a lesbian had affected their relationship with their adoptive parents or family, while two asserted that their sexual identity and being a lesbian had not affected their relationship with their adoptive parents and family. Some of the women felt that their sexual identity and being a lesbian had initially negatively affected their relationship with their adoptive parents or family, but eventually improved it. One woman stated:

> She (adoptive mother) is as accepting as she can be with (partner). In her deepest heart of hearts, she would love to see me with a man. It never gets said anymore. I know it's hard, particularly around the issue of grandchildren. I'd like to have a child, and I know it's hard for her (adoptive mother) to accept two women having children. She can't tell anybody. Look, this is a picture of my son-in-law. She's not like, Oh this is my daughter's lesbian lover. So I think it's socially difficult for her.

For some women the conflict with their adoptive parents was more pronounced:

> One of the reactions my mom had with it (me coming out as a lesbian) was, It couldn't have happened with me (adoptive mother). It has nothing to do with me (adoptive mother). This is you (lesbian who is adopted). We (adoptive parents) didn't

raise you to be that way (lesbian). I did not disagree with her. What I always thought was it's very interesting that I think I've come as a package of haves and that I arrived as a complete person to be with parents and brothers. We were raised in the same environment and we are as diametrically opposed as three people can be. I know that being adopted is a part in parcel of the whole thing and being a lesbian is part in parcel of the whole thing. All entwined, intertwined.

As the respondents reflected on the relationship between their lesbianism and their status as adopted persons, differing sets of connections were expressed. In the quote that follows, the respondent highlights the importance of her lesbian relationship in feeling comfortable and secure with the new discovery of herself.

I never really found that I had the difficulty of coming out or with the idea of being adopted, because I've had a relationship the whole length of time that I've been out (as a lesbian). I'm comfortable and secure. I don't see it (sexual identity and being a lesbian) connecting with adoption issues in any conflicting way.

Another women identified a biological connection to lesbianism (born as a lesbian):

I don't think it (being adopted) has anything to do with my sexuality. I feel that my sexuality is rooted in my parents. I think it (being a lesbian) would have come out if I hadn't been adopted.

Another woman identified her relationship with her adoptive mother as an influencing factor in her sexual orientation.

I have something I firmly believe in, based upon various factors on having and not having. I think that female affection and connection with my mother helped push me in the direction towards lesbianism, because she was not at all that type of person. She didn't even want to touch. She was the sort of person who did not show any type of affection or love. Yeah, I think it (adoption) had a great factor on my being a lesbian.

Lesbian Community

The respondents were divided in their perceptions of the importance of lesbian community; half found their participation in lesbian groups vital to their identity and comfort level. The others expressed either a neutral stance or dissatisfaction with lesbian community.

A woman who found another adopted lesbian in the lesbian group she joined, expressed that the connection with this person, on the basis of their shared status as adopted lesbians, was empowering.

Adoption Support Groups

Some adopted lesbians have found adoption support groups helpful in resolving identity-related issues. The lesbian adopted persons interviewed for this paper expressed the opinion that there is a need for adoption support groups exclusively of lesbians. Some of the women who had joined support groups felt that the group did not welcome an exploration of their concern related to their sexual orientation and, in some instances, rejected and chastised them. They responded to the rejection by quitting the group. One woman expressed interest in networking with other adopted lesbians and wished for a structure that would make that possible.

As stated before, adopted lesbians have two closets to come out of in the process of total identity acceptance. Most of the respondents found the adoption closet more difficult to come out of than their lesbian closet. This response might be a reflection of the fact that the majority of the women who responded to the invitation to be interviewed for this paper got the information through their participation in events of the lesbian community. All of the women expressed interest in seeing more written about lesbians who are adopted, as a way of ending their invisibility and of helping them to come out of the adopted closet.

When asked to give advice to other adopted lesbians, the women offered the following kinds of advice:

> I guess it would be the advice that was given to me–to go on and be angry. To come to terms with it and let it go because

you don't self-actualize until you do that. You don't know who you are when you have that wall of anger. With the adoption situation, I think there is definitely something missing and I don't know if it causes it or it helps it along. There are many complexities, and anger. Seek help and try to let it go because there are so many questions about yourself and your being that you can't allow that hostility to be there and stay there if you want to understand yourself, so just basically try to work it out. I guess for everyone to struggle with whatever their issues are there maybe is a gain in the similarities (of being a lesbian and adopted), but find what's meaningful (for yourself) in the adoption and lesbian experience. I'd be happy to share my experiences if that would help somebody, if they were feeling like they needed to hear. I don't know what one could say, except that one could listen and acknowledge that these are difficult issues, from the depth of what it all means. I would certainly encourage people in treatment (to seek help) in their love affairs and relations with other people to find true meaning.

DISCUSSION

Perhaps one of the most prominent conclusions of this paper is that an overwhelming majority of the lesbians who were adopted and were interviewed for this study felt more comfortable with their lesbian identity than with their adoption issues.

For example, the majority of these lesbians who were adopted had come out as lesbians and were active in the lesbian community, to greater or lesser degrees. However, most of the lesbians represented in this study had not actively discussed their adoption issues with their adoptive families. Many of these women also had not joined a support group and thus felt isolated from and uninvolved in the adoption community.

This study points to a possible need for adoption support groups that focus on the issues of lesbians who are adopted. Many of the women who were interviewed expressed interest in joining a support group for lesbians who are adopted.

For those who were adopted before six months of age, the adoption experience was positive and nonconflictual. However, women adopted closer to one year old or older tended to consider the adoption experience as a shame-based issue, and as something that was not discussed openly by their adoptive families, either during their childhood or adulthood. For these women, disappointment and shame were part of their negative baggage of being adopted. A question that needs further exploration is why all women found it more difficult to even discuss their adoptive status than their lesbianism, and why this difficulty was also operative within the context of their adoptive families.

This situation might be based on the fact that the women in the study were adults and adoption was secretive in the '50s and '60s when these women were adopted. A follow-up study to explore these issues with lesbians adopted when the veil of secrecy had begun to lift might provide alternative insights into this issue.

My inquiry identified that loyalty issues played a role in the subjects' lack of action in searching for birth parents/family. Loyalty to the adopted family contributed to feelings of deep sadness and regret on the part of some subjects for not searching for their birth mothers.

Searching is helpful in understanding the reasons for being relinquished for adoption and thus easing the pain of rejection and self-blame for this rejection. Fantasies about birth parents, particularly birth mothers, are also coping techniques often used by the subjects to resolve feelings of rejection by their birth families.

It is clear that the stigma of adoption bears more heavily on lesbians than the stigma of lesbianism. One might speculate that lesbian identity is greatly an adult task, while adoptive identity is a childhood task. Adoptive issues seem to be more related to the core of "who am I?" by linking the questions to "whose daughter am I?", while lesbian identity relates more to "who I want to share my life with."

Issues related to intimacy, fear, and trust are of crucial importance to all lesbians since we do not have the legal protection that heterosexuals have when they establish intimate relations through the institution of marriage. Lesbians enter intimate relations fully aware that the law will not protect them if their mutual trust is violated, including not only emotional issues but also financial ones. Adopted lesbians who felt secure as children, because the law legitimized their family structure, are denied that same level of comfort and legitimacy when they establish a new family as adults in a lesbian relationship.

In coping, adopted lesbians might be more reluctant to end an unhealthy relationship because of their historical experience of having felt abandoned by their birth families. They might see themselves as "rescuers" of their partners, duplicating the same rescue that they experienced when adopted. Adopted lesbians found it easy to include lesbian friends as part of their family network. This might be based on the fact that early in life they realized that family was based more on relationship than on blood ties.

My study stems from my personal commitment to integrate the many aspects of my identity in a wholeness that strengthens and empowers me and all women of color. Being a Korean adopted lesbian social worker helped me identify a void in the professional literature that is of importance if the profession is going to effectively serve an increasing number of actual or potential clients. Feminist standpoint theory validates the notion of using marginal experiences as a central part of mainstream inquiry and practice, enriching that inquiry and practice.

My personal life story, summarized in the following article, further illustrates the conclusions discussed in this paper.

REFERENCES

Andujo, E. (1988). Ethnic identity of transethnically adopted Hispanic adolescents. *Social Work, 33*, 531-535.

Baer, J. (1990-1991). *Chain of life newsletter.* Berkeley, CA: Chain of Life.

Boston Lesbian Psychologies Collective. (1987). *Lesbian psychologies: Explorations and challenges.* Chicago, IL: University of Illinois Press.

Bruining, A.M. (1990). Made in Korea: A feminist perspective on Korean adoptions in the U.S. *Sojourner, 5*(June) 15-17.

Caplan, L. (1990). *An open adoption.* New York: Farrar, Straus & Giroux.

Chapman, B.E., & Brannock, J.C. (1987). Proposed model of lesbian identity development: An empirical examination. *Journal of Homosexuality, 14*(3/4), 69-80.

Chesler, P. (1988). *Sacred bond: The legacy of Baby M.* New York: Random House.

Deeg, C. (1990). Defensive functions of the adoptee's cathexes of the lost object. *Psychoanalysis and Psychotherapy, 8*(2), 145-156.

Deeg, C. (1991). On the adoptee's search for identity. *Psychoanalysis and Psychotherapy, 9*(2), 128-133.

Gilligan, C. (1982). *In a different voice: Psychological theory and women's development.* Cambridge, MA: Harvard University Press.

Gilman, L. (1977). *The adoption resource book.* New York: Harper & Row.

Humphrey, H., & Humphrey, M. (1989). Damaged identity and the search for kinship in adult adoptees. *British Journal of Medical Psychology, 62*(4), 301-309.

Kim, D.S. (1978). Issues of transracial and transcultural adoption. *Social Casework, 59*(8) 477-486.

Kowal, K.A., & Schilling, K.M. (1984). Adoption through the eyes of adult adoptees. *American Journal of Orthopsychiatry, 55*(3), 354-362.

Lifton, B.J. (1988). *Lost and found: The adoption experience.* New York: Harper & Row Publishers.

Lukes C., & Land, J. (1990). Biculturality and homosexuality. *Social Work, 35,* 155-161.

MacCowan, L. (1987). Review of "the 'new gay' lesbians" by Lillian Faderman. *Journal of Homosexuality, 14*(3/4) 173-178.

Margolies, L., Becker, M., & Jackson-Brewer, K. (1987). Internalized homophobia: Identifying and treating the oppressor within. In Boston Lesbian Psychologies Collective (Ed.). *Lesbian psychologies: Explorations and challenges* (229-241). Chicago, IL: University of Illinois Press.

Marquis, K.S., & Detweiler, R.A. (1985). Does adopted mean different? An attributional analysis. *Journal of Personality and Social Psychology, 48*(4), 1054-1066.

Monteflores, C., & Schulz, S.J. (1978). Coming out: Similarities and differences for lesbians and gay men. *Journal of Social Issues, 34*(3), 59-72.

Reber, A.S. (1985). *Dictionary of psychology.* New York: Penguin Books.

Rosenweig-Smith, J. (1987). Factors associated with successful reunions of adult adoptees and biological parents. *Child Welfare, 57*(5), 411-422.

Sachdev, P. (1991). Achieving openness in adoption: Some critical issues in policy formation. *American Journal of Orthopsychiatry, 6*(12), 241-249.

Sochoberg-Winterberg, T., & Shannon, J. (1988). Adoption and adult psychosocial adjustment. *Social Work, 33,* 17-19.

Sophie, J. (1987). Internalized homophobia and lesbian identity. *Journal of Homosexuality, 14*(1-2), 53-65.

Stein, T.S., & Cohen, C.J. (Eds.). (1986). *Contemporary perspectives on psychotherapy with lesbians and gay men.* New York: Plenum Publishing Corporation.

Troiden, R. (1988). Homosexual identity development. *Journal of Adolescent Health Care, 9,* 105-113.

Troiden, R. (1989). The formation of homosexual identities. *Journal of Homosexuality, 17*(1-2), 43-73.

Woolf, H.B. (Ed.) (1972). *The Merrian-Webster Dictionary.* New York: Simon & Schuster.

A Few Thoughts from a Korean, Adopted, Lesbian, Writer/Poet, and Social Worker

Mi Ok Bruining

SUMMARY. The struggle to construct identity is an ongoing process. Three questions can be understood as shaping that process: "Where did I come from?" "Who am I now?" and, "Where am I going?" This article illustrates the process of identity constructions within the framework offered by those questions, from the standpoint of a Korean, Adopted, Lesbian, Writer/Poet.

People ask me why I decided to become a social worker. There are many reasons–all reflecting the elements in the title of this paper. My reasons for becoming a social worker might be better explained if I provide some of my own "herstory."

I was born in (South) Korea, in 1960, The Year of the Rat, and lived in an orphanage for the first five years of my life. In Korea, the "War" is known as the "American War," and in it thousands of Korean children were orphaned. In 1966 at the age of five I was adopted by a U.S. white family. My adoptive family lived in New Jersey and later moved to Rhode Island just before I started high school. From 1979 to 1983, I attended art school in Virginia, but did

Mi Ok Bruining, MSW, is a Social Worker, Social Work and Discharge Planning Department, Beth Israel Medical Center, New York, NY.

[Haworth co-indexing entry note]: "A Few Thoughts from a Korean, Adopted, Lesbian, Writer/Poet, and Social Worker." Bruining, Mi Ok. Co-published simultaneously in *Journal of Gay & Lesbian Social Services* (The Haworth Press, Inc.) Vol. 3, No. 2, 1995, pp. 61-66; and: *Lesbians of Color: Social and Human Services* (ed: Hilda Hidalgo) The Haworth Press, Inc., 1995, pp. 61-66; and: *Lesbians of Color: Social and Human Services* (ed: Hilda Hidalgo) Harrington Park Press, an imprint of The Haworth Press, Inc., 1995, pp. 61-66. Multiple copies of this article/chapter may be purchased from The Haworth Document Delivery Center [1-800-3-HAWORTH; 9:00 a.m. - 5:00 p.m. (EST)].

61

not graduate or obtain a degree. In 1984, I moved to Boston and lived there for six years. While there I decided to reenter college in 1987, and completed my B.A. in Creative Writing in Vermont in 1989. Shortly after graduation I relocated to New York City and six months later I decided to go for my M.S.W. I entered the first and only social work program I applied to, and the one that accepted me.

I graduated in 1992, after two and a half years of stressful, intensive, grueling, full-time studying, moving six times, three different places to live, three different relationships, having three different cars, and sinking myself into enormous debt. Needless to say, I experienced many changes–both logistic and emotional. One year later, I am currently employed as a hospital social worker in Manhattan.

Being adopted has always been a predominant issue for me. As an adopted member of a typical Wonderbread white, upper middle-class protestant adoptive family, I benefitted from many obvious economic and (seemingly) social privileges. I rode horses since I was six, and competed in horse shows with my own horse for eleven years. I vacationed in the country with my family, and was given all of the material objects I needed and wanted. I lived in New Jersey with a family of three older, white, non-adopted siblings, and two white parents. I was surrounded by white classmates, in a white neighborhood. Later I lived in a rural New England town where I was the only Korean adolescent, and attended a high school where I was the only Korean student.

My childhood and adolescence were filled with constant overt and covert experiences of racism. These experiences included the subtle stares of young children, name-calling by older children, verbal harassment, and verbal threats of violence, which at one time escalated into an incident of stone-throwing by older adolescents. Adults often asked (and still ask) offensive, intrusive and inappropriate questions.

These years of racism, in the form of verbal abuse, ostracism, and blatant hatred caused profound psychic wounds and scars. The repercussions of society's intolerance and rejection of my Asian appearance were internalized feelings of alienation, rage, despair, sadness, self-hatred and self-loathing, low esteem, and loneliness. As a child, I felt I was on a planet of one. When I attempted to share my feelings with my parents, they were unempathic, and often contributed to my pain with their own form of racism and ignorance. My parents had poor insight and still do not acknowledge the psychic damage caused. As a child and adolescent, I internalized my rage and pain, and split into two; my outside behavior reflecting an extroverted, athletic, seemingly well-adjusted individual with many friends. On the inside I was in angst, felt like a total freak, an outsider, and often prayed and wished at night before falling asleep that I would not wake up in the morning, but would fade away peacefully. I was deeply depressed for many years, but did not realize it until I was twenty-something. I always knew something was wrong, but was never able to name it. I know now, that many of the feelings I had were related to the fact that I was adopted; some were normative emotions having to do with the torturous emotional agony of adolescence.

I was a Korean person in a white family, and lived in a white community, in a country and society that reinforces white culture. Until my twenties, I socialized with only white peers, and had no mirroring role models or mentors who were Asian. In my adoptive family, I was constantly conditioned by and brainwashed with racist stereotypes of Asians and I never saw one positive representation of Asian people on television or in a film. In grade and high schools, I was taught that people of color were inferior to white people.

In art school I discovered that I did not want to be a commercial artist/illustrator. I refused to resign myself to creating airbrushed illustrations of mundane objects, and did not love painting and printmaking enough to accept the role of a starving artist, hoping someday to be "discovered." I left art school, bitter, cynical, depressed, and zapped of all my passion to draw. I lost my creativity and it was years before I drew a drawing for myself, for the pure joy of drawing. The one spark of passion that ignited for me while I was at art school was creative writing. I took a poetry writing class for the first time, and fell in love with words. The idea of being able to create pictures with words, and to evoke emotions with words excited me in the way that drawing excited me when I discovered at the age of six, that I had artistic talent. I believed that I always saw things differently. Now I could write about it.

In 1984 I returned to Korea for the first time since I had arrived in the U.S. eighteen years before. I toured Korea for two weeks. It was a painful, but also very healing experience, and very necessary for my survival. The experience resolved some old issues and created some new ones for me. When I returned from Korea, I began working at a nondescript retail job in Boston just to pay the rent. I joined Asian American organizations, an Asian women's group, became politically active in the Asian American community, and met very strong, very powerful, smart, progressive Asian women and other women of color. I fell in love with an Asian woman for the first time, and began accepting speaking engagements on issues of international adoptions. The first few years in Boston were intoxicating and exhilarating. Finally, I was able to understand the oppression, conditioning, lies, myths, and marginalization I had felt all of my life. I was able to name it all, and my rage surfaced. I channeled this rage into writing, artwork, political activities, organizing, and public speaking. I was often unemployed between times of working at an international adoption agency, temping for several weeks to several months at a time, doing short-term bicycle messenger work, and finally working at a state human services agency two and a half years. At this agency I learned American Sign Language (ASL).

I felt I could identify with deaf people's struggle at not being understood by insensitive hearing people and the dominant (hearing) culture's refusal and unwillingness to accept deaf culture. I felt that all of my life I, too, had not been understood or accepted.

In 1987, after several relationships with women, I came out to myself as a lesbian. Two years later, I came out to everyone who was of significance in my life, including my family. Once I was out of the closet, I was so relieved! I realized that my reluctance and fear about coming out stemmed from the fact that being a lesbian represented yet one more identity issue that I would be forced to struggle with. Actually coming out was healing, liberating and reaffirming for me. Since then, I have been active in Asian Pacific lesbian organizations, and cultivated important friendships with other Asian Pacific lesbians and other lesbians of color.

My parents were and still are homophobic, but I have made it clear to them that I visit them less often because they have not accepted my sexual identity. It makes me very sad, but I feel that their homophobia is their problem. We communicate regularly, but my lesbian relationships are something that I do not share with them. My parents' attitude is similar to the nauseating "Don't Ask, Don't Tell, and Don't Hold Hands" Policy.

While finishing my undergraduate studies in Vermont, I was the token Asian lesbian on campus and in the writing program I was enrolled in; yet, at the same time I had a very strong support network of Asian lesbians in Boston. I was thrilled to have the exciting opportunity to work with fierce, creative, brilliant, revolutionary-minded women writers and poets, such as Bernice Mennis and Irena Klepfisz. Shortly after I completed my B.A. I began graduate school at Smith College School for Social Work. I felt that I had a strong understanding of the macro issues, but no understanding of the micro issues–in a clinical context. One of the reasons I selected Smith was because of its strong clinical program. I completed two and one-half years at Smith, with two five-days-a-week/nine-month field placements, three ten-week summers of course work, and a masters thesis, entitled, "Whose Daughter Are You? Exploring Identity Issues of Lesbians Who Are Adopted."

In graduate school I learned a great deal about myself and social work. I explored my role as a social worker and as a mental health professional. I learned more about macro systems and micro issues. I studied social policy, community organizing, hierarchy in agencies, pathology, diagnosis, treatment of patients and clients, and research. I developed my technical writing skills. Smith, like most or all other social work programs, is a microcosm of the greater society in the U.S.A. One does not experience there an abundance (if any) of sensitivity to those who differ from the cultural "norm." I must admit, as cynical and realistic as I claim to be, that I was genuinely disappointed by this discovery.

I have completed over forty national and international speaking engagements in the last ten years, and continue to be invited to address the economic, political, social, racist, cultural, and clinical issues of international adoptions in the U.S.A. I have had twenty poems and several articles published. More recently, I have been doing local and regional invitational poetry readings, and I am working on completing two books, a collection of poems, and an article on issues of international adoptions.

I have a strong network of friends, and a wonderful, funny cat named Fiona. I look forward to the time when I have four things that will help make my life complete: a decent place in which to live, a rewarding job, a reliable car, and a healthy, committed relationship. I have continued to struggle with profound loneliness.

As a Korean, adopted, lesbian, poet/writer, and trained social worker, I do not *represent* each group I identify with; rather I offer my contribution as an individual member of each group with my distinct opinions, experiences, and commitment in my creative, political, personal, social and professional environments.

I am short in height (I prefer "vertically-challenged") and left-handed (I prefer "right-brained attuned"). Humor is a powerful defense, and can be very entertaining at times. I have been ostracized, misunderstood, oppressed, marginalized, and discriminated against–as a woman, an activist, and Asian person, a woman of color, and as a lesbian of color.

Whenever I work with a patient or client–whoever s/he may be, despite her/his homophobia, racism, hatred or whatever negative behavior towards me, I want to try and find something tender and gentle, some element of strength and dignity, some redeeming quality in her/him, and latch onto it with as much empathy and connectedness as I can. Sometimes, it is a challenge and a struggle to do this, yet I believe empathic attunement, communication and listening are vital skills of a social worker. As a human being and as a social worker, I am still under construction.

The Social Service Need of Lesbians of Color

Mary E. Swigonski

SUMMARY. The social service needs of lesbians of color are complex because of multiple oppressions. Their needs are ambiguous because the coping abilities of many lesbians of color can mask those needs. This article reports the findings of an exploratory study of social workers' perceptions of the social service needs of lesbians of color. The findings of that study are analyzed from the standpoint of lesbians of color as articulated within their writing. That writing highlights the struggle for personal wholeness, political visibility, and social justice within multiple, often conflicting cultures. The need for sociocultural structural change is emphasized.

The social service needs of lesbians of color are complex and ambiguous. Their needs are complex, because lesbians of color have the same needs for services as every other human being, as well as additional needs because of the multiple oppressions that confront them. The social service needs of lesbians of color are ambiguous, because the ability of lesbians of color to cope under the worst conditions, can mask their need for material support, empowerment, and liberation.

Mary E. Swigonski, PhD, ACSW, is Assistant Professor, Social Work Department, Rutgers, The State University of New Jersey Campus at Newark, 360 Dr. Martin Luther King Jr. Blvd., Newark, NJ 07102. Her research interests include feminist standpoint theory and its implications for social work research and for practice and program evaluation.

[Haworth co-indexing entry note]: "The Social Service Needs of Lesbians of Color." Swigonski, Mary E. Co-published simultaneously in *Journal of Gay & Lesbian Social Services* (The Haworth Press, Inc.) Vol. 3, No. 2, 1995, pp. 67-83; and: *Lesbians of Color: Social and Human Services* (ed: Hilda Hidalgo) The Haworth Press, Inc., 1995, pp. 67-83; and: *Lesbians of Color: Social and Human Services* (ed: Hilda Hidalgo) Harrington Park Press, an imprint of The Haworth Press, Inc., 1995, pp. 67-83. Multiple copies of this article/chapter may be purchased from The Haworth Document Delivery Center [1-800-3-HAWORTH; 9:00 a.m. - 5:00 p.m. (EST)].

On a daily basis, lesbians of color are targeted as Black, female and lesbian, each of which is, or may be affected by class (Gomez, 1993). As early as 1979, the Combahee River Collective (1983) noted the interlocking nature of oppressions, and argued against ranking or prioritizing oppressions. Barbara Smith (1983) succinctly articulates that analysis: "We examined our lives and found that everything out there was kicking our behinds: race, class, sex, and homophobia. We saw no reason to rank oppressions." Smith (1983) then catalogues some of the issues and needs that lesbians of color have been working on:

> [R]eproductive rights, equal access to abortions, sterilization abuse, health care and child care, the rights of the disabled, violence against women, rape, battering, sexual harassment, welfare rights, lesbian and gay rights, educational reform, housing, legal reform, issues related to women in prison, aging, police brutality, labor organizing, anti-imperialist struggles, antiracist organizing, nuclear disarmament, and preserving the environment.

Ida Red (1982) notes that public activism for lesbians of color must include "custody rights, state rights, employment rights, federal rights, religious rights, parade rights, and coalition rights."

Given this complexity of the life circumstances of lesbians of color, and given the importance of accurate needs assessment for effective social work intervention, social workers' perceptions of those needs constitute a critical foundation for the beginning of practice intervention. A review of the social work practice literature identified no studies in this area. To begin to address this issue, an exploratory study was conducted. This paper reports the findings of that pilot study of social workers' perceptions of the needs of lesbians of color, and discusses those findings from the standpoint of lesbians of color as articulated in their writings.

THE STUDY

Methods

A questionnaire was mailed to 175 social workers from an east coast (New York-Philadelphia) metropolitan area. The questionnaire consisted of a cover letter explaining the nature of the study, an informed consent form, a demographic information sheet, and a three-page survey form. Each page of the survey form focused on one particular ethnic group: African-Americans, European-Americans (white people), and Latino Americans. The focus of the study was limited to three groups to manage the amount of information requested from respondents. These three groups were chosen because they represent the three largest groups within this geographical area.

Respondents were asked to "list five to ten of the human service needs that you believe are most important for . . . " Respondents were asked to complete a separate listing for each of six groups: African-American lesbians, African-American gay men, European-American lesbians, European-American gay men, Latina lesbians, and Latino gay men. This article focuses its discussion on the social workers' articulation of the needs of lesbians of color.

Names of social workers were secured from alumni associations, membership lists from several community agency task forces, and resource lists published by gay and lesbian groups. Of the 175 questionnaires mailed, about 25 were returned "Undeliverable/ Moved." Twenty-one questionnaires were returned completed for about a 14% completion rate.

This completion rate reflects the nature of mail surveys, which suffer from low completion rates in general. A particularly low completion rate was anticipated for this study, given the open-ended nature of the questions asked, the amount of time and thought required to complete the questionnaire, and the emotionally charged nature of the topic. (Several recipients of the questionnaire, who phoned the author, demanded to know how that person's name and address were secured for "that kind of research.") However, the completed responses do provide preliminary data with which to formulate an understanding of professionals' perceptions of the needs of this population.

Of the 21 persons completing the survey, 13 were European Americans, 8 were people of color; 15 were women, 6 were men; 8 were gay men or lesbians, and 13 were heterosexuals. All respondents held at least a master's degree in social work or a related discipline, and were currently engaged in direct practice for more than one year in their current job.

Because of the preliminary nature of this study, responses were simply grouped together to form as comprehensive a list as possible of social workers' perceptions of the needs of lesbians of color. This procedure is comparable to the first step in the Delphi Survey Procedure (Johnson, Meiller, Miller, & Summers, 1987; McKillip, 1987).

Results

The needs listed by the respondents have been grouped into five categories: material, identity, relationship, loss or threatened loss, and cultural and social change.

Material Needs

Respondents to the survey listed the following basic material needs for lesbians of color: food, housing/real estate, financial assistance and financial management skills. Respondents also suggested the importance of career counseling and employment or job training. The need for assistance in becoming self employed/or starting one's own business was also identified. Health care needs were highlighted, including the need for health education and information regarding breast cancer, and obstetrical and gynecological issues. The need of lesbians of color for access to educational opportunities and financial aid was identified. The need for reduced fee child care and reduced fee services in general, as well as general information and referral services, were also noted.

Identity Needs

Respondents to the survey indicated their awareness of the multiple assaults on the development of a sense of identity for lesbians of color. They indicated the need for both gay and ethnically sensitive service providers, who should convey both general support and acceptance. The need to help lesbians of color develop their sense of self-esteem and self-acceptance within this context was indicated.

The need for support in the "coming out" process and concerning internalized homophobia were also noted. Consciousness raising was suggested as an important resource. The need for particular care, guidance and support of teenagers and young adults who are beginning to confront their lesbianism, including school-based programs, was identified by respondents.

Relationship Needs

Survey respondents identified the need of lesbians of color for support and counseling within a range of relationships, including: lovers or partners, family of origin (both nuclear, and extended), and family of procreation. Respondents suggested that services might be helpful for some lesbians of color who find themselves struggling with enmeshment in new relationships. The need for assistance with parenting issues (related to birth children, adoptive children, and foster children) was recognized, along with the need for supportive services to help single mothers. The need of families of lesbians for counseling and support was also noted.

Additionally, respondents highlighted the importance and need for peer, companionship, support networks. The importance of an entertainment and meeting center, where lesbians of color could freely meet, was also suggested.

Loss/Threatened Loss Needs

Respondents to the survey displayed sensitivity to many of the forms of discrimination that lesbians of color face, through the areas of loss and threatened loss that they identified as human service needs for these women. Examples of some (but clearly not all) of these losses include loss of employment, loss of heterosexual friends, loss of family, loss of standing in community at large and ethnic community in particular, loss of children if a parent, and the potential loss of life through lesbian bashing. Their recognition of the pervasiveness of these losses is indicated in the recognition for the need of stress management, and a variety of support groups (including identity and affinity groups, survivors of incest and abuse groups, and twelve step programs).

Respondents also named specific kinds of programs they believed to be essential to many lesbians of color. Those included sexual abuse programs, drug and alcohol treatment programs, domestic violence programs, and protective services. The need for sex education, including safer sex information and AIDS prevention and treatment, were also highlighted. Additionally, the general need for crisis intervention, supportive services, and support groups was also identified.

Responses within the survey also began to develop a brief catalogue of the multiple oppressions that confront lesbians of color. The need to reduce and eliminate institutional racism was emphasized. Related to that, the need for programs to help lesbians of color to manage hostile environments was acknowledged. Homophobia and racism were specifically identified as shaping the hostile environment of lesbians of color (although sexism was not identified). Within that context the need for protection from, and services related to, gay bashing, and police harassment and neglect were listed.

Respondents also noted the difficulties lesbians of color may face in child custody battles, and other court cases attempting to claim their civil rights. The needs for affordable and competent legal services and support around these issues were named.

The only life cycle specific area that manifested in the survey responses was the need for services that specifically address elderly lesbians of color.

This list of potential and actual loss related needs paints a rather grim picture. However, it is still not a comprehensive representation of the kinds of social and interpersonal losses that threaten lesbians of color. O'Leary (1978) catalogued the specific kinds of discrimination that threaten all lesbians. The following discussion is based on that work. She noted that beyond the discrimination we face as women, lesbians encounter many legal problems in this country because the laws of our land discriminate unjustly on the basis of sexual or affectional preference. Gay men and lesbians may not marry the person they love. Gay men and lesbians are routinely denied government employment in many areas, turned down for security clearances, cashiered out of the armed forces, rejected as immigrants, denied custody of their own children, taxed at higher rates, and excluded from the benefits of many social programs.

There are also an abundant variety of extralegal discriminations, by individuals, that are barred when it comes to other minorities, yet are widely sanctioned in both law and social attitudes when it comes to gay men and lesbians. In most parts of the country employers are free to fire or refuse to hire otherwise qualified persons merely because they are gay; property owners may refuse to rent, lease, or sell to gays; and operators of public accommodations may declare their establishments off-limits to "overtly" gay customers. O'Leary detailed these areas of discrimination in 1978. Fifteen years later, the list stands as valid with few modifications. New Jersey and a few other states have passed laws banning discrimination against gay men and lesbians, but these laws have yet to be tested.

While the recent presidential election promised the hope of an end to discrimination in the military, the now proposed "don't ask, don't tell" solution stands as a violation of the First Amendment guarantee to free speech. The exchange of one area of discrimination for another is not a gain. Lesbians need equal standing within the law and protection of civil rights through the law.

Cultural and Social Change

Respondents indicated the needs of lesbians of color for both cultural support and social change. The need for cultural programs and exchanges to create an accepting climate within which lesbians of color can more safely live was noted. Respondents also identified the need for the development of programs that support reciprocity of acceptance by lesbians of color: the acceptance of lesbians of color by their families, as well as the acceptance of lesbians of color, their culture, values, family, and language by the dominant society.

Respondents also indicated their awareness of the importance of spirituality and/or religion for many lesbians of color. They highlighted the need for services that attend to the spiritual needs of these women, and for sensitivity and openness by religious groups to their needs.

The need for programs to create the conditions for social equality was affirmed by survey respondents. Two specific social changes that were highlighted were the creation of equal employment opportunities that include nondiscriminatory practice in the workplace, and the legalization of marriages for lesbians of color (as well as for white lesbians and all gay men).

Respondents also highlighted the need for services that include empowerment, coalition building, and advocacy. There was a clear recognition of the need to eliminate legal discrimination against lesbians of color. There was also a recognition of the need for political action to end discrimination through legislation and to support equal rights. Respondents also highlighted the need for building multi-focus coalitions across the lines of color, ethnicity and sexual orientation.

The need for the education of the public and of community organizations was also highlighted. Areas of noted educational need included gay/lesbian lifestyle, orientation vs. lifestyle choice; and more inclusive definitions of family. Additionally, the need for education about the characteristics and effects of racism and sexism, and how they divide our communities was indicated. Respondents also highlighted the need for research programs to better understand the lesbian community, and to combat AIDS.

Reflecting on this fairly extensive list of sociocultural, interpersonal and individual needs, it becomes clear that there are two roots feeding these sets of needs: lesbians of color share the common human needs that emerge from the day-to-day lived reality of the human condition; lesbians of color are also confronted with an additional set of needs emerging from the multiple and interlocking oppression they confront in the forms of racism, sexism, and heterosexism (and frequently classism). The survey responses indicate an awareness on the part of respondents to the common human needs of lesbians of color, and an awareness of some needs related to specific aspects of oppression. But there was not a clear indication of the unique needs experienced by lesbians of color as a result of the interlocking nature of the multiple oppressions that confront them. How is being a lesbian of color different from being a white lesbian, or being a person of color? The literature of lesbians of color provides an answer to that question.

DISCUSSION

Given the multiple and interacting effects of oppression in the lives of lesbians of color, and given the fact that many of the respondents to the survey were not lesbians of color (only one respondent was), additional sources of information were sought, sources in which lesbians of color speak for themselves. In reviewing the literature on lesbians of color, it is remarkable to note the dearth of material published by or about them in the "mainstream" social work journals. The scope of the search was then expanded to include journals targeted to gay and lesbian life, and a few articles were identified. But to obtain any material of substance, it was necessary to expand the circle of the search to include sources that target persons of color, particularly anthologies edited by women of color. If European-Americans are going to understand lesbians of color, it is necessary to search for materials outside the traditional circle of European-American social work literature.

Four sites of struggle for lesbians of color emerge from the literature written by these women: lesbian invisibility, the development of a sense of identity, conflicts with community and family of origin, and conflicts with white society. These sites of struggle will provide the framework for the discussion of the needs of lesbians of color from their standpoint.

Lesbian Invisibility

The nature of lesbian oppression is not the same kind of domination/subordination relationship that characterizes many other forms of oppression. Lesbian oppression is more accurately characterized as an erasure. Lesbians can ostensibly "choose" to avoid the more visible consequences of discrimination by staying in the closet, by remaining invisible. Gay people have been invisible to historians. There are virtually no records of the accomplishments and social contributions of gay men and lesbians (white or of color). When someone questions why lesbians and gay men want to "come out," when someone objects to lesbians or gay men showing affection in a public place, they are in fact suggesting that lesbians and gay men do not (or should not) exist.

Ethnic minority lesbians and gay men are rarely acknowledged as part of the homosexual community, or racial ethnic community in which they live and function (Morales, 1990). Nothing in the Chicana culture nor in the dominant culture validates or even acknowledges lesbian existence (Gaspar de Alba, 1993). The sociopolitical analysis of many white feminists saying that heterosexism is the primary or even sole oppression that lesbians face denies the existence of lesbians of color and other groups that are affected by other forms of oppression such as ageism, classism, anti-semitism and ableism (Kanuha, 1990).

Folayan (1992) points out that all of the descriptions of lesbian that she had heard or read were clearly about white women. For her, lesbian, like French or Swedish, was a word that referred to people who were white. The vast majority of material written about lesbians has nothing to do with an individual as a woman of color. Folayan points out that she grew up in a cultural vacuum. She reminds us that it is hard to get knowledge about who you are and where you come from when everyone around you is completely ignorant of who you are.

Identity

Ethnic lesbians and gays live in three rigidly defined and strongly interdependent communities: the gay male and lesbian community (white), the ethnic minority community, and the society at large. It requires a constant effort to maintain oneself in three different worlds, each of which fails to support a significant aspect of the person's life (Morales, 1990). It's not possible to be proud of oneself without a fairly clear definition of who one is. One must feel positive about one's identity (Gock, 1992). For lesbians and gay men this means integrating multiple identities including sexual orientation, gender, race, ethnicity. Making the choice to be queer is an empowering act, an act of self-definition and rebellion (Gaspar de Alba, 1993).

Audre Lorde (1982) remembered how being young and Black and gay and lonely felt. "A lot of it was fine, feeling I had the truth, and the light and the key. But a lot of it was purely hell. There were no mothers, no sisters, no heroes. We had to do it alone, like our sister amazons, the riders on the loneliest outpost of the kingdom of Dahomey. Always we moved in a necessary remoteness that made

'What did you do this weekend?' seem like an impertinent question."

Asian-American identity is still critically bound to claiming the right to exist (Aguilar-San Juan, 1993). The Asian-American lesbian must confront not only homophobia but also racism in her claim to multiple identities and to making herself whole. The conflicting self-identification of lesbian Asian-Americans is reflected in several factors, including the choice of a community of identification and the choice of terms (does the individual perceive herself as an Asian-American lesbian, or as a lesbian Asian-American?), situational factors such as the level of outness, and perceptions of how one is viewed by one's several communities of association (Chan, 1989).

Being a Native lesbian is like living in the eye of a hurricane: terrible, beautiful, filled with sounds and silences, the music of life affirmation, and the disharmony of life despising (Brant, 1993). Faced with homophobia from their own communities, faced with racism and homophobia from the outsiders who hold semblances of power over them, Native lesbians profoundly feel the desire to connect. Within this context naming oneself as lesbian becomes a significant act of love and community. "To balance, to create, in the midst of this is a gift of honor. . . . Taking words learned from the enemy and beading them together and making a gift of beauty is a giveaway of lasting love" (Brant, 1993, p. 947).

Lesbians of color suffer from the duality that says they are able to be only one or the other. It claims that human nature is limited, and cannot evolve into something better (Anzaldua, 1987). Anzaldua asserts, "I, like other queer people, am two in one body, both male and female. I am the embodiment of the hieros gamos, the coming together of opposite qualities within . . . It is an interesting path, one that continually slips in and out of the White, the Catholic, the Mexican, the Indigenous, the instincts, in and out of my head." For Anzaldua, and for lesbians of color, this is a path of knowledge. La Mestiza copes by developing a tolerance for contradictions and for ambiguity. It is a way of balancing, of mitigating duality. Lesbians of color must interpret the multiple cultures that spawned them. This is a spawning born of struggle, domination, and anger (Anzaldua, 1987). Lesbians of color are always engaged in the process of self creation.

Conflict with Community of Origin

The existence of a group of women who live and thrive independently of men suggests that sexism as an institution has not been effective in controlling all women (Kanuha, 1990). The existence of a group of women who live and thrive independently of men suggests that the men have failed to control "their" women. Lesbians of color, women who live and thrive, independently of men, are a threat to the male community.

In Asian cultures, being gay is frequently viewed as a rejection of the most important roles for women and men: that of being a wife and mother for women, and that of being a father for men (Chan, 1989). Carrying on the family line for procreation is a particularly important role for men. Family is valued as the primary social unity throughout the person's life. And the most important obligation, especially as a son, is the continuation of family through marriage, and the bearing of children. If the son or daughter is gay, the implication is that not only has the child rejected the traditional roles of wife/mother, or son/father, but also that the parents have failed in their role, and that the child is rejecting the importance of family in Asian culture.

For the lesbian of color the ultimate rebellion she can make against her native culture is through her sexual behavior. In affirming her lesbianism, she goes against two moral prohibitions: sexuality and homosexuality (Anzaldua, 1987). In the Chicano community, because she rejects the traditional roles ascribed to women in patriarchal Mexican culture (the roles of wife, mother virgin, or whore), she fails to participate in propagating the race or serving the macho. Because of this threat to her culture, the Chicana is marginalized within her own culture.

Many lesbians and gay men have to leave their families, communities, and churches to find home (Gutierrez, 1992). Even when integrated within their own family and community it is usually as an honorary heterosexual, rather than as an out and acknowledged lesbian of color.

Lesbians of color are perceived as a threat to both white society, and their communities of origin. They receive mixed messages from their communities of origin about their status within it. In the Puerto Rican culture, as most cultures, values relating to sexual behavior and sexual roles are practiced zealously by the middle class, however, the lower and upper classes are more easily exonerated for transgressing these codes of behavior (Hidalgo and Christensen, 1976-77). The poor and working-class Black community has often tolerated an individual's lifestyle prerogatives, even when that lifestyle was disparaged by the prevailing culture (Clark, 1983). Lesbians and gay men may have been exotic subjects of curiosity, but they were accepted as part of the community and neighborhood.

For Native lesbians, the impact of the conflict with white society has been particularly severe. Historically, gay men and lesbians were highly regarded within Native cultures. The majority of Native peoples classified people as having more than two genders. Lesbians and gay men are frequently referred to as two-spirited. Two-spirited is not primarily a sexual orientation, but a spiritual/social identity. The offices and duties of gays and lesbians included teaching, keeping the knowledge of the elders, healing, child care, spiritual leadership and participation, herbal wisdom, interpretation of spirit messages, mediation, and artistic expression (Grahn, 1986; Tafoya, 1992).

The two-spirited peoples were often the first Indians killed by Europeans, even when the tribes were tolerated by white people. For example, the explorer Balboa set wild dogs on the homosexual medicine men of California, killing them (Tafoya, 1992). Christian missionaries worked with American Indians with the mandate to "civilize" them. The missionaries accomplished this through the forced segregation of children in boarding schools, depriving them of access to their culture (Tafoya, 1992).

Conflict with White Society

Lesbians of color have a particular set of needs in relationship to white society. Anzaldua (1987) declares that lesbians of color need to say to white society that they need white society to acknowledge its reaction to and negation of lesbians of color. They need white society to own the fact that they looked upon them as less than human. They need white society to own the fact of stealing their lands, their personhood, their self respect. On behalf of lesbians of color, Anzaldua calls on white society to make public restitution. She calls on white society to acknowledge that in order to compensate for a sense of defectiveness, members of white society strive for power over people of color. White society erases the history and experience of people of color, because remembering makes white society feel guilty. Anzaldua challenges members of white society to acknowledge that they split themselves from minority groups, that they disown such groups; that members of white society split off parts of themselves, transferring the "negative" parts onto persons of color. She summons white society to affirm its fear and its distancing through masks of contempt (Anzaldua, 1987, p. 86). Finally, Anzaldua invites members of white society to tell lesbians of color what the members of white society need from lesbians of color.

Lesbians of color also have a set of needs in relationship to white women. "The racial solidarity and privilege among white people, which maintains the institution of racism, allows many white lesbians the free choice to dissociate themselves from men, on the basis of lesbian and gender identity. However, due to racism and the concomitant need for people of color to bond together against it, lesbians of color are inextricably bound to their racial ethnic communities and therefore to men of color" (Kanuha, 1990, p. 172). Ethnicity and feminism are not at war with each other, yet women of color are often made to feel that they must make a choice between them (Yamada, 1981). The failure of white lesbians to recognize this need on the part of lesbians of color creates an unnecessary conflict between the two communities.

Summation

Being a lesbian of color in this country is not easy. For lesbians of color the combined effect of racism in lesbian and feminist communities, and sexism and internalized oppression in communities of color is often silencing (Kanuha, 1990). Yet, the greatest disappointments and painful experiences of the lesbian of color, if she makes meaning of them, can lead her toward becoming more of who she is (Anzaldua, 1987, 1990). In addition to struggles for personal wholeness, and political visibility, lesbians of color need to think constructively about the rest of society and how to create peace, justice and sexual freedom in our lifetimes (Aguilar-San Juan, 1993).

CONCLUSION

This paper began with a discussion of an exploratory pilot study of social workers' perceptions of the needs of lesbians of color. Five general kinds of needs were identified by respondents to the survey: material, personal and group identity, loss and anticipated loss, relationship, and social and cultural change. The writings of lesbians of color identify similar, although somewhat different kinds of needs. The difference is one of focus and emphasis: survey respondents emphasized material and interpersonal needs, while the writings by the lesbians of color emphasized the need for change in the social structure. Lesbians of color speak of the need to be visible. They speak of their need to create an identity from the multiple cultures that spawn them. They speak of their need to resolve the conflicts with their communities of origin, and to reclaim their roles within them. Lesbians of color speak of their need for social change and the end of oppression at the hands of white society. Lesbians of color speak of their need for a free and just world. Lesbians of color speak of their need for social workers to take seriously our commitment to social justice and social action.

Social workers need to carefully hear the voices of lesbians of color, to respond with them to create a world where it is safe to be visible, together creating a free and just world.

REFERENCES

Aguilar-San Juan, K. (1993). Landmarks in literature by Asian American lesbians. *Signs, 18*(4), 936-943.

Anzaldua, G. (1987.) *Borderlands/La Frontera: The new Mestiza.* San Francisco: Spinsters/Aunt Lute.

Anzaldua, G. (1990). Bridge, drawbridge, sandbar or island. In L. Albrecht & R. M. Brewer (Eds.). *Bridges of power: women's multicultural alliances* (pp. 216-231). Santa Cruz, CA: New Society Publishers.

Brant, B. (1993). Giveaway: Native lesbian writers. *Signs, 18*(4), 944-947.

Chan, C. S. (1989). Issues of identity development among Asian-American lesbians and gay men. *Journal of Counseling and Development, 68,* 16-20.

Clark, C. (1983). The failure to transform: Homophobia in the Black community. In B. Smith (Ed.). *Home girls: A Black feminist anthology* (pp. 197-208). New York: Kitchen Table/Women of Color Press.

Combahee River Collective. (1983). Combahee River Collective statement. In B. Smith (Ed.). *Home girls: A Black feminist anthology* (pp. 272-282). New York: Kitchen Table/Women of Color Press.

Folayan, A. (1992). African-American Issues: The Soul of It. In B. Berzon (Ed.). *Positively gay: New approaches to gay and lesbian life* (pp. 235-239). Berkeley, CA: Celestial Arts.

Gaspar de Alba, A. (1993). Tortillerismo: Work by Chicana lesbians. *Signs, 18*(4), 956-963.

Gock, T. S. (1992). Asian-Pacific Islander issues: Identity integration and pride. In B. Berzon (Ed.). *Positively gay: New approaches to gay and lesbian life* (pp. 247-252). Berkeley, CA: Celestial Arts.

Gomez, J. (1993). Speculative fiction and black lesbians. *Signs, 18*(4), 948-955.

Grahn, J. (1986). Strange country this: Lesbianism and North American Indian tribes. *Journal of Homosexuality, 12*(3/4), 43-57.

Gutierrez, E. S. (1992). Latino issues: Gay and lesbian Latinos. In B. Berzon (Ed.). *Positively gay: New approaches to gay and lesbian life* (pp. 240-246). Berkeley, CA: Celestial Arts.

Hidalgo, H. A. & Christensen, E. H. (1976-77). The Puerto Rican lesbian and the Puerto Rican community. *Journal of Homosexuality, 2*(2), 109-121.

Johnson, D. E., Meiller, L. R., Miller, L. C. & Summers G. F. (1987). *Needs assessment: theory and methods.* Ames, IA: Iowa State University Press.

Kanuha, V. (1990). Compounding the triple jeopardy: Battering in lesbian of color relationships. *Women & Therapy, 9*(1/2), 169-84.

Lorde, A. (1981). The master's tools will never dismantle the master's house. In C. Moraga & G. Anzaldua (Eds.). *This bridge called my back: Writings by radical women of color* (pp. 98-101). Watertown, MA: Persephone Press.

Lorde, A. (1982). *Zami a new spelling of my name: A biomythography.* Freedom, CA: The Crossing Press.

McKillip, J. (1987). *Need analysis: Tools for the human services and education.* Applied Social Research Methods Series, Volume 10. Newbury Park, CA: Sage Publications.

Morales, E. S. (1990). Ethnic minority families and minority gays and lesbians. *Journal of Homosexuality, 8,* 217-239.

O'Leary, J. (1978). Legal problems and remedies. In G. Vida (Ed.). *Our right to love: A lesbian resource book* (pp. 196-203). Englewood Cliffs, NJ: Prentice Hall, Inc.

Red, I. V. S. W. (1982). Notes on "reading a subject" in periodical indexes. In M. Cruikshank (Ed.). *Lesbian studies: Present and future* (pp. 162-164). Old Westbury, NY: The Feminist Press.

Smith, B. (1983). *Home girls: A black feminist anthology.* New York: Kitchen Table/Women of Color Press.

Tafoya, T. (1992). Native gay and lesbian issues: The two-spirited. In B. Berzon (Ed.). *Positively gay: New approaches to gay and lesbian life* (pp. 253-260). Berkeley, CA: Celestial Arts.

Yamada, M. (1981). Asian Pacific American women and feminism. In C. Moraga & G. Anzaldua (Eds.). *This bridge called my back: Writings by radical women of color* (pp. 71-75). Watertown, MA: Persephone Press.

Lesbian Latinas:
Organizational Efforts to End Oppression

Mariana Romo-Carmona

SUMMARY. Organizational efforts in the Latino community during the last ten years have contributed positively to the self-image of Latina lesbians and gay men, have given them affirmative role models, and have helped end feelings of isolation. The author documents the pattern and organizational style implemented, a pattern based on the cultural norms of Latinos, and demonstrates how this pattern was instrumental in bringing about positive acceptance of Latina lesbians and gay men by their families. The integration of Latino lesbian and gay organizations with other Latino organizations addressing problems facing the whole Latino community is emphasized. Finally, the next steps to be taken in the collective struggle are identified.

DEL OTRO LADO

. . .

She remembers
The horror in her sister's voice
'Eres una de las otras',
The look in her mother's face as she says

Mariana Romo-Carmona is Co-Editor, *Cuentos: Stories by Latinos*, Kitchen Table Press, 1983, a member of the Editorial Collective Conditions, 1988, recipient of the Lesbian Fiction Award from Astraea Foundation, 1991, and Managing Editor, *Colorlife*, New York City.

[Haworth co-indexing entry note]: "Lesbian Latinas: Organizational Efforts to End Oppression." Romo-Carmona, Mariana. Co-published simultaneously in *Journal of Gay & Lesbian Social Services* (The Haworth Press, Inc.) Vol. 3, No. 2, 1995, pp. 85-93; and: *Lesbians of Color: Social and Human Services* (ed: Hilda Hidalgo) The Haworth Press, Inc., 1995, pp. 85-93; and: *Lesbians of Color: Social and Human Services* (ed: Hilda Hidalgo) Harrington Park Press, an imprint of The Haworth Press, Inc., 1995, pp. 85-93. Multiple copies of this article/chapter may be purchased from The Haworth Document Delivery Center [1-800-3-HAWORTH; 9:00 a.m. - 5:00 p.m. (EST)].

85

'I am so ashamed, I will never
be able to raise my head in this pueblo'
The mother's words are barbs digging into her flesh.
De las otras. Cast out. Untouchable.

'But I am me', she cries, 'I've always been me'
'Don't bring your queer friends into my house,
my land, the planet. Get away.
Don't contaminate US, get away'.

Away, she went away.
But every place she went
they pushed her to the other side
and that other side pushed her to the other side
of the other side of the other side
Kept in the shadows of other.
No right to sing, to rage, to explode.
. . .

–Gloria Evangelina Anzaldua (1987)[1]

The excerpt from Anzaldua's poem captures the stigma, the rejection, the "not belonging" of lesbians of color. It speaks of our invisibility, of our rage.

Laura S. Brown (1989) defines lesbian reality as being informed by biculturalism, marginality and normative creativity. The intent of this paper is to illustrate how Latina lesbians have used biculturalism, marginality and normative creativity to heal and empower themselves. In this process of healing and empowerment, "coming out" and organization have been essential tools to achieve our goal.

I present a developmental case history of the Latina lesbian community in the city of New York. I have been an active participant in this developmental process that involves individual as well as collective actions and growth. Thus, the case history is written from my standpoint.

A DEVELOPMENTAL CASE HISTORY
OF LATINA LESBIANS

In 1993 there are young Latinas in the City of New York who, while going through the process now known as "questioning one's sexuality," go looking for an organization of Latina lesbians for someone to talk to. And it is not only younger women, but also recent Latin American immigrants, who go through the Gay Yellow Pages or ask at the women's bars, or demand from the Lesbian Switchboard that someone direct them to a social or support group for Latina lesbians.

What is significant about this is not simply how far we have come in ten years, but that these transformations apply in the Latino/a community as well as in the Anglo community. Ten years ago a Latina lesbian would have been the only Latina, possibly the only woman of color, at a support group telling her coming out story. She would have been isolated in her neighborhood, at her job or at school, and she would have dreaded the next Navidad she would have to spend without her lover.

Today she may turn on El Show de Christina[2] and watch Latina lesbians talking (in Spanish and English) about issues that concern our community. She may watch Latina lesbians on TV, sitting with her Mami (mother) on the sofa and planning whether to make the pasteles at Titi's (aunt's) house or at her lover's apartment this year. What's more, if she is a recent immigrant, she can go to the Lesbian Health Fair next spring, and find information on breast cancer, all written in Spanish by other Latina lesbians. And next summer, she can attend the Puerto Rican Parade up Fifth Avenue and see a contingent of Lesbian and Gay Latinos/as marching with information on HIV or AIDS.

Of course, this mythical Latina can only represent the difference between being part of the social makeup of this city, and not being on the map at all. Racism is not gone and neither is homophobia. But the institutionalization of certain groups and organizations in the City has certainly changed the landscape and the expectations of people with regards to what they expect from the social fabric, and therefore from social services. We are just at the beginning of these changes, but the changes are dramatic. I think we can see them most clearly in our community because here, the Latina lesbian has made inroads into a most unchangeable system: the family. And she has done it with her own presence.

Speaking as an activist looking at these changes, I am often more pessimistic because the work I do starts on the side of what has to be done. And from this side, it looks as though we have barely scratched the surface. Nevertheless, the history of a Latina lesbian presence in this area has come about precisely the way social change needs to happen: from the bottom up, or should we say, from the inside out. Latina lesbians have been involved in grass-roots groups during the social activism of the 60s, at a time when the white mainstream gay movement was fledgling and focusing more exclusively on gay issues; i.e., of concern mostly to white gay men and some white lesbians. Because of this, Latina lesbians were invisible in their communities as well as in the gay community.

The women who eventually moved on to be clearly visible as Latina lesbians were also active in Latin American feminist organizations, in pro-Puerto Rican independence and Latin American solidarity movements, labor, the Left, reproductive rights, human rights, housing, anti-racist movements, as well as lesbian and gay rights. In New York City, this broad political consciousness existed before Latinas were ready to organize specifically as Latina lesbians, but in other cities in this country, Latinas were already identifying the need to organize specifically as Latina lesbians.

In 1986, Las Buenas Amigas was formed in New York to serve as a bridge to Latin American lesbians who were, at that time, planning the first lesbian Encuentro in Mexico. In Boston and Los Angeles, Latinas had been organized as lesbians since the early 80s, while in Texas, Latinas formed organizations before the Encuentro in Mexico in 1987.

The way that women organized was to create networks rather than large, formal organizations. In fact, many women have been resistant to the tradition of top-heavy organizations that make burdensome demands on their members.

In most cities where there has been an initial "gay and lesbian Latinos" organization, the lesbians soon split off to form their own autonomous groups. So, while Las Buenas Amigas worked to create a space for Latina lesbians in New York, they are also connected with women in Los Angeles, San Francisco, Chicago, Miami, Houston, Dallas, Hartford, and Boston.

The First Encuentro de Lesbianas de Latino America y El Caribe took place in Cuernavaca, Mexico in October 1987. The Second took place in San Jose, Costa Rica, in April 1990, and the Third in

Cabo Rojo, Puerto Rico in August, 1992. Meanwhile, the fact that a Latina lesbian can travel almost anywhere in Latin America and the United States, and reach some part of a network of lesbian feminist solidarity, also reinforces her presence at home.

Latina lesbians are an intrinsic part of the lesbian and gay political scene in New York City. Las Buenas Amigas formed part of the Lesbian and Gay People of Color Steering Committee, a coalition of groups that share resources and support, coordinate activities, and wield a great deal of power and influence in the political arena. Each year, Latina lesbians join in the Lesbian and Gay Pride March in New York, as well as in the Puerto Rican Parade, as part of a contingent of lesbian and gay people. The Puerto Rican Parade is a unifying event for all the Latin American communities in the city, not just Puerto Ricans, and it is significant that since 1989 the parade's officials have permitted the lesbian and gay contingent to register and to march. Although there have been people along the march route who have yelled disparaging taunts and homophobic remarks, the overall reaction to the presence of open lesbians and gay men has been positive. In 1979, when a small contingent from the Comte Homosexual Latino Americano (C.H.O.LA.) marched in this parade, the response was more violent and onlookers threw chunks of bread, beer cans and other projectiles at the marchers, threatening further violence and resulting in only two or three marchers completing the march. This inclusion in events is significant because Latin Americans have traditionally been accused of being more homophobic than other ethnic groups, yet few could deny that the recent behavior of a great number of Irish people at the St. Patrick's Day Parade tends to belie this assertion.

Another contribution of Latina lesbians to our communities has been the publication of *Compañeras: Latina Lesbians* (Ramos, 1987). This anthology of essays, short fiction, poetry, oral histories and interviews, comprises the first collective statement and testimonial to our existence. Because this book enjoys wide distribution in universities, at conferences, and mainstream bookstores, the impact has again been to change expectations as to where and how Latina lesbians are portrayed.

DISCUSSION

The multiple marginality of Latina lesbians contributes to increase the empowering effect of coming out. "Coming out" by the least powerful, most oppressed members of a society challenges the foundation of power, by individuals whom the power structure considers to be the least threatening. This rebellion of the least powerful elicits acts of retaliation and punishment from the powerful elite and their agents of social control.

Historically, lesbians of color compartmentalized and prioritized the multiple levels of oppression they experienced rather than integrating them in their efforts to end oppression. This compartmentalization and prioritizing directed their efforts to address racism and economic marginalization first. In doing this they stayed in the closet and remained silent to their oppression as women and lesbians.

Active participation in the civil rights movements of the sixties and seventies served as a training ground for Latina lesbians, many of whom were in leadership positions in these organizations. Their participation in these organizations also helped them achieve recognition and respect from the Latino community and from progressive "straight" Latinos in civil rights organizations.

The next growth step followed: Latina lesbians began an integrated analysis that linked the many systems of oppression that affected their lives. "Coming out" individually and collectively became a matter of survival of themselves as "whole" individuals.

"Coming out" for Latinas is difficult, dangerous and contagious. It is a never-ending process. In coming out the Latina must negotiate (1) her Latina cultural roots and the dominant Anglo culture in which she now lives and works (both cultures share a heterosexist, patriarchal norm), (2) her marginality that puts her always "on the other side" in whatever social structure she is interacting/participating in at any given time, (3) her normative creativity that stems from a standpoint experience that has helped her survive and achieve "contra viento y marea" (against all odds).

For Latinas, "coming out" started in the family unit: in this "coming out" Latinas faced the most difficult dilemma: losing the support of the one group in which they were not "en el otro lado" (on the other side).

Hidalgo (1987) and Hidalgo and Christensen (1979) studied the process of Puerto Rican lesbians "coming out" to family, friends and coworkers. Hidalgo reports, "Family acceptance or tolerance, rather than rejection of homosexual members, was related to the overall tone existing in the family relationship. Where the family was warm, with close ties of understanding for all its members, the homosexual member was not singled out for rejection" (Hidalgo, 1984). Hidalgo (1984) documents changes in the reaction and behaviors of family members toward lesbians and gays in their families. Her 1984 study reported more acceptance and tolerance of lesbians and gay family members than her 1979 study (Hidalgo & Christensen, 1979). She attributes individual "coming out" to families as very significant in changing the homophobic behaviors in Puerto Rican families.

Individual acts of "coming out" prepared the way for collective and public "coming out." Latina lesbians started "coming out" in print. "Coming out" is an act of birthing ourselves within our culture. . . . becoming alive.

In my introduction to the book *Compañeras: Latina Lesbians* (Ramos, 1987), I speak of the empowering effects of our collective coming out.

> The issue of being able to express the meaning of our lives is an important one for Latina lesbians because as lesbians, we are seen mainly through our sexuality. Coming out means that we stake out our ground, and we claim that territory for ourselves both as Latinas and as Lesbians, whole persons who live and work in the context of a community. . . . But the women we really are can only live if we break the secret. Saliendo del closet is ultimately helping to create support for all that we are, to create a Latina lesbian community. (Romo-Carmona, 1987)

While some of us have been able to heal and empower ourselves through the coming out process and through participation in Latina and Latino lesbian and gay organizations, much remains to be done.

THE NEXT STEP

Giving an overview of the impact of Latina lesbians in our communities is simply that, an overview. What is missing is that within the Latina lesbian community there are a great many women who have not been reached by our networks and continue to be isolated. At the same time, the nature of community groups, support networks, political organizations, and social services is defined by the people who form them. This means that these structures are not accessible to all Latina lesbians, i.e., class, race, and educational level continue to play a part in how we organize.

What is also missing are youth-run and youth-defined groups for Latina lesbians. While young Latinas can attend meetings and participate in activities organized by existing groups, there are no spaces where Latinas under 20 years of age, who have just come out or are questioning their sexuality, can gather and address their own issues as they define them. There are also no counseling resources for young women, no health care resources that meet the needs of young women, no employment and training options for young Latina lesbians or bisexual women. The most serious omission is perhaps health care for Latinas with HIV, particularly for women who sleep with women but who don't identify as lesbians. Most social service agencies that deal with HIV in the Latino/a communities simply approach the delivery of services from a heterosexist standpoint. We need only look at the intake questionnaires and look at the questions related to sexual activity, to confirm that this is so. Most service providers fail to look at the family situations of Latina lesbians by assuming that a woman with children is not a lesbian. In order not to jeopardize receiving services, a lesbian would be forced to conform to the expectations of the social services system, thereby obliterating evidence that she, her lover, and their children exist.

It is for all of these reasons that Latina lesbian activists attempt to move the civil rights agenda to address the issues of daily living. This is necessary in order to live as whole persons.

The tasks remaining are clearly overwhelming, yet the impact that Latina lesbians have had upon our communities is impressive. We may begin to see in the years to come that we have helped to

bring our communities along to another stage, toward a more humane, less heterosexist and homophobic community, a community in which "being out" does not make us "Del Otro Lado."

NOTES

1. Excerpts of a poem. Reprinted with permission.
2. El Show de Christina is a syndicated T.V. show that is broadcast by Spanish-speaking stations in Massachusetts, Connecticut, New York, New Jersey, Pennsylvania, Florida, New Mexico, Texas, California, Illinois, Puerto Rico, Peru, Panama and Republica Dominicana.

REFERENCES

Anzaldua, G. E. (1987). Del otro lado. In J. Ramos (Ed.), *Compañeras: Latina lesbians, 1st ed.* (pp. 7-8). New York: Latina Lesbian Project.

Brown, L. S. (1989). New voices, new visions, toward a lesbian/gay paradigm for Psychology. *Psychology of Women Quarterly, 13,* 445-458.

Hidalgo, H. & Christensen, E. H. (1979). The Puerto Rican cultural response to female homosexuality. In E. Acosta-Belen (Ed.), *The Puerto Rican woman* (pp. 48-63). New York: Praeger.

Hidalgo, H. (1984). The Puerto Rican lesbian in the United States. In T. Darty & S. Potter (Eds.), *Women-identified women* (pp. 105-117). Palo Alto, CA: Mayfield Publishing Company.

Hidalgo, H. (1987). Fuera del closet, Boricua. In J. Ramos (Ed.), *Compañeras: Latina lesbians, 1st ed.* (pp. 25-29). New York: Latina Lesbian Project.

Ramos, J. (Ed.) (1987). *Compañeras: Latina Lesbians, 1st ed.* New York: Latina Lesbian Project.

Ramos, J. (Ed.) (in press). *Compañeras: Latina Lesbians, 2nd ed.* New York: Rutledge Press.

Romo-Carmona, M. (1987). Introduction. In J. Ramos (Ed.), *Compañeras: Latina Lesbians, 1st ed.* (pp. 1-4). New York: Rutledge Press.

Being Pro-Gay and Pro-Lesbian in Straight Institutions

Cheryl Clarke

SUMMARY. Understood within the context of black consciousness, lesbianism is an opportunity to challenge the prevailing power system. But, being Black, queer, feminist, and "marvelous" is complicated by the spaces ahead and the spaces behind. For example, one's commitment to "lifting while we climb,"[1] necessitates asking: "Where (else) am I climbing and who (else) am I lifting?" "Taking an anti-heterosexist stance" is encouraged as a proactive and preventive strategy in this work. The goal of this work is decentering of heterosexuality and heterosexual privilege, unhinging and changing the power dynamics of sexual politics in this culture.

Lesbianism became an option for me when I realized that lesbianism includes politics, not simply "lifestyle": a powerful alternative to conventional female roles; and that Black lesbians existed in fact and in history. These realizations enabled me to "come out" from the first, with relatively no time in the closet. Lesbianism became a choice for me–not destiny, fate, or biology. As a child of the 1960s who experienced the Black Power Movement and the

Cheryl Clarke, MSW, is Director of Diverse Community Affairs and Lesbian Gay Concerns at Rutgers, The State University of New Jersey, and author of *Narratives: Poems in the Tradition of Black Women* (1982); *Living as a Lesbian* (1986); *Humid Pitch* (1989); and *Experimental Love* (1993).

[Haworth co-indexing entry note]: "Being Pro-Gay and Pro-Lesbian in Straight Institutions." Clarke, Cheryl. Co-published simultaneously in *Journal of Gay & Lesbian Social Services* (The Haworth Press, Inc.) Vol. 3, No. 2, 1995, pp. 95-100; and: *Lesbians of Color: Social and Human Services* (ed: Hilda Hidalgo) The Haworth Press, Inc., 1995, pp. 95-100; and: *Lesbians of Color: Social and Human Services* (ed: Hilda Hidalgo) Harrington Park Press, an imprint of The Haworth Press, Inc., 1995, pp. 95-100. Multiple copies of this article/chapter may be purchased from The Haworth Document Delivery Center [1-800-3-HAWORTH; 9:00 a.m. - 5:00 p.m. (EST)].

power of black consciousness, lesbianism was an opportunity to challenge the prevailing power system which awards privilege to exclusive and compulsory heterosexuality.

After my volatile coming to consciousness as a Black person, i.e., confronting my status as an African in diaspora, coming out as a lesbian was far less painful and far less fraught with ambivalence. I had gained practice challenging white skill privilege. Feminism had caused me to understand and challenge my subordinate status as a woman. However, I had far less practice challenging sexism, which is often more difficult to illuminate and was often subsumed in the energy used to challenge racism. As a person who lives with multiple identities I have experienced the difficulty of neutralizing multiple oppressions simultaneously.

Once a British journalist asked James Baldwin, in his early years, if it were not a burden for him to be both "Negro and homosexual." Baldwin, smiling broadly, responded, "Why no, I think it's marvelous!" I always enjoy recalling that answer when my family, friends, or colleagues come at me with arguments of double and triple jeopardy and advise me against being too much of a "public homosexual."

While my experiences of blackness, lesbianism, and feminism have empowered me, I realize my experiences are not universal. I have certain luxuries, even as a woman who is a member of a "despised 'race'." First and foremost, I have, for 24 years, worked in a public institution of higher education, albeit straight, white, and male-dominated (the dastardly triumvirate), among people who have respected me, where the life of the mind is theoretically cherished and where I have been able to be out politically–as a Black person, a feminist, and a lesbian. So, I have not had to lead a double life for fear of losing my job, my children, or my housing. On the other hand, claiming these identities or rather using these identities as strategies for social change, has not been without its costs and responsibilities, e.g., the sometime ostracism from other Black professionals, loss of credibility with students, and lack of promotion earlier in my career in student affairs.

Historically, Black people in the U.S. have not had the luxury to be individualist, i.e., doing for self and self alone. In the words of Mrs. Josephine St. Pierre Ruffin and the other 19th century Black feminists, we have had to be "lifting as we climb" (Lerner, 1973, p. 433). Now, as patronizing as that might sound, I bought (and still buy) into this notion that I, and other Black people in similar positions, have the responsibility to bring others along, to hold the doors (of opportunity) open for others of my race coming after me. I do believe that I am somewhat of an inheritor of DuBois' (1989, p. 87) theory of the "talented tenth." Therefore, like the undaunted Mrs. St. Pierre Ruffin and the vaunted Dr. DuBois, I, too, have my missions. But being Black, queer, feminist, and "marvelous" in a post-secondary education institution, in the era of late capitalism, in a post-modern world, is not only complicated by the space ahead, but just as much by the space behind. Where (else) am I climbing and who (else) am I lifting?

I fear that this piece is too self-referential. But I am a feminist and I do take my own subject position seriously. The question of multiple identities in the human service arena is the great challenge awaiting us as human service providers at the dawn of the 21st century, whatever our settings and disciplines. Call it diversity. Call it multiculturalism. Call it cross-cultural relations or the demographic revolution. One thing is certain, we have all been called as witnesses.

Gloria Anzaldua (1990, p. 383), Latina lesbian writer and witness, says that whatever the "blood" (read as "race," "ethnicity," "culture"), homosexuality (queerness) cuts across all "color lines." Queerness is not to be reified, only seen as one of the many signifiers in the matrix we call multiculturalism. Education is desperately needed. Straight human service providers have almost as much at stake as queer human service providers, particularly as we face the anti-sex beliefs, practices, and discourses that have such virulent currency at present.

Queers are everywhere and so are homophobes (and heterosexists)! They aren't only on the Joint Chiefs of Staff. Self-referentially and mindful of my survival, I argue for lesbian, gay, bisexual perspectives, i.e., I argue for a critique of, a decentering of heterosexuality and heterosexual privilege in the context of human service delivery. As I said above, lesbianism is not solely an identity; it is also a strategy–a way for me to get my political work done. I come out as a lesbian to educate people and make heterosexuals less secure about their hegemony just as much as to express my "right" to love women. Being anti-heterosexist–whether or not one is gay, lesbian, bisexual, i.e., queer–works the same way: entering as an anti-heterosexist human service provider in a multicultural world, institution, agency, setting.

As an educator and student affairs administrator who works with undergraduate leaders and professional staff, I have encouraged a set of assumptions called, "Taking an Anti-Heterosexist Stance." Taking an anti-heterosexist stance involves a kind of proactiveness and preventiveness. In order to subvert the presumption of hetero-sexuality and to be inclusive of diverse perspectives, assume that in any group gay, lesbian, bisexual people are present. Once you have assessed the risks, let it be known that you are an anti-heterosexist person and that you welcome the contributions of persons of all sexual orientations, preferences, choices, identities. Whatever your sexual practice or preference, interrupt anti-gay or anti-lesbian comments, jokes, stereotypic pronouncements on the part of peers, colleagues, and clients. Language is extremely important. So, use the terms gay or "lesbian" when referring to persons who, over time, are involved in same-sex sexual-affectional relationships. Refrain from using the term "homosexual" to describe the communities of lesbians and gay men. Persons who are heterosexual never refer to themselves as such, though heterosexuality takes up much space, time, and energy. Sexuality is one part of the politics of lesbian-gay liberation: we are not only fighting for the "right" to sleep with who we want to but for the opportunity to fashion a future, to shape events, to influence the world as proud lesbian-gay-bisexual people. Although we have done this, often it has happened at the expense of who we are.

Lesbians and gay men have many differences, not the least is marked by gender construction. Gay men enjoy male privilege even though they are oppressed by heterosexism. Lesbians are oppressed by both sexism and heterosexism. Both communities have distinct cultures and histories. Lesbians, gays, and bisexuals of color have different and differing perspectives from our counterparts. Often we do not wish to leave or isolate ourselves from our cultural/racial communities, even though we have endured painful experiences because of our communities' homophobia and heterosexism. We have multiple identity issues and tend to view sexuality or sexual practice with more fluidity than some of our white counterparts. Often we understand the stance of bisexuality as a space of negotiation of identities and preferable to what we see as the rigidity of a lesbian or gay identity. We have the dual responsibility of educating our communities as well as the straight white world.

Learn what you can about lesbian and gay cultures–they do exist. Do not become distracted from your anti-heterosexist work when people accuse you of being gay or lesbian because you have taken a stand against anti-gay and anti-lesbian beliefs and practices. Remember: whites who supported and struggled for Black civil rights were called "nigger lovers." Accept your own gay, lesbian, and bisexual potentials, even if you never act upon them.

Respect a gay, lesbian, or bisexual friend's, colleague's, client's, or student's decision to come out or to be private about his/her sexual identity. Be cautious about identifying lesbian, gay, or bisexual persons to others in any situation, even to other gay people, unless you are certain the person wishes his or her identity known. Refrain from speculating about people's sexual orientation in the work setting– such speculation is inappropriate in most settings and can be dangerous in straight environments. If your sexual practice is heterosexual, understand your privilege and the ways in which heterosexuality is rewarded in this culture. If you are in a helping relationship with a gay, lesbian, or bisexual person, be able to make appropriate referrals for services like psychotherapy, HIV/AIDS testing or counseling, lesbian-sensitive women's health care, or non-traditional health care services. Because an institution can be straight, i.e., square, rigid, exclusionary, elitist, in more than its expression of hegemonic heterosexuality, it is important that heterosexism be contextualized by other oppressions, e.g., racism, sexism, anti-Semitism, ableism.

Lesbian and gay liberation is a broad struggle, expanding beyond the issue of civil rights. Our work, like the work of feminists, is also to unhinge and change the power dynamic of sexual politics in this culture, not merely to be accepted into the military or the church.

It is important not to become dogmatic about your anti-heterosexist practice. Thus, a certain amount of fluidity and flexibility is encouraged, especially as information and people change almost daily.

NOTE

1. "Lifting as We Climb," the motto of the National Association of Colored Women. NACW formed in 1896 when the National Federation of Afro-American Women and the National League of Colored Women united.

REFERENCES

Anzaldua, G. (1990). La conciencia de la mestiza: Towards a new consciousness. In G. Anzaldua (Ed.). *Making face/making soul: Hacienda caras* (pp. 377-389). San Francisco: An Aunt Lute Foundation Book.

DuBois, W.E.B. (1989). Of the training of Black men. *The souls of Black folk* (pp. 62-76). New York: Penguin Books (originally published in 1903).

Lerner, G. (Ed.). (1973). *Black women in White America: A documentary history*. New York: Vintage Books.

Index

Ableism, 76
Activism, by lesbians of color, 68
Adolescent lesbians
Latina, 92
support and education programs
for, 71
Adolescents, adopted, 47
Adopted lesbians
lesbian identity development
issues of
adoptive and sexual identity,
54-55
adoptive parents/family, 51
attitudes towards adoption,
51,52-53
attitudes towards lesbian
community, 56
birth parents/family, 54
coming out, 51,52,54-55,57
motherhood status, 51
relationship issues, 50-51,59
search for birth parents/family,
52,53,58
support group membership,
45,56-57
therapy/counseling
experiences, 51
personal narrative by, 61-66
support groups for, 45,56-57
Adopted persons, identity and
psychosocial development
of, 47-48
Adoption
"closed," 46
cross-cultural, 46
personal narrative of, 61-66
definition of, 45
"open," 46

parental rights in, 45-46
Advocacy, for lesbians of color, 74
African-American children,
cross-cultural adoption of, 46
African-American community, lack
of homophobia in, 79
African Americans, "passing" by, 24
Ageism, 76
Alliance work, 16-17
American Psychiatric Association, 1
American Public Health Association, 1
Anthologies, of works by lesbians of
color, 15,20-21,89
Anti-semitism, 76
Asian-American lesbians
conflict with traditional values, 78
identity development by, 77
"passing" by, 24
personal narrative by, 61-66
Association of Black Social Workers,
46
Attachment, in female identity
development, 44

Balboa, Vasco Nunez de, 79
Biculturalism, of Latino lesbians, 86
Biography, interpretative, 28-29
Boston, Latina lesbian community
in, 88
Buenas Amigas, Las, 88,89

Caregiving, female, 9
Chain of Life newsletter, 45
Chicago, Illinois, Latina lesbian
community in, 88
Chicana culture, 76

Child custody, 72-73
Civil rights movement, 88,90,92
Classism, 10,76
    of human service organizations, 4
Coalitions, of lesbians of color, 74
Combahee River Collective, 68
Coming out
    by adopted lesbians,
        51,52,54-55,57
    components of, 48-49
    by Latina lesbians, 86,90-91
    by lesbians of color, 71
    professionally, 1,2,4
    as reaction to homophobia, 44-45
    relationship to identity
        development, 48
Community of origin, of lesbians of
    color, 78-79
Companeras: Latina lesbians, 89,91
Compartmentalization, by lesbians of
    color, 90
Comte Homosexual Latino Americano
    (C.H.O.L.A.), 89
Council on Social Work Education, 30
Creativity, 14,15
    normative, 86,90
Cultural identity, 48
Cultural programs, for lesbians of
    color, 73

Dallas, Texas, Latina lesbian
    community in, 88
De Otro Lado (Anzaldua), 85-86
Diaries, of lesbians of color, 15
Difference, concept of, 14-15
Discrimination
    homophobic, 72-73
    preferred sameness model of, 3
    racist, 1
    sexist, 1
    towards lesbians of color, 72
Dominance, relationship to
    heterosexism, 9-10
Dominant culture, oppression by, 8-9

Elderly lesbians, of color, 72
El Show de Christina, 87
Empathy, 12-13
Employee benefit policies,
    homophobic discrimination
    in, 23-24
Employment, homophobic
    discrimination in,
    23-24,73,74
Empowerment
    of adopted lesbians, 56
    of adopted people, 47,56
    of Latina lesbians, 86,91
    of lesbians of color, 74
    relationship to gay/lesbian
        identity development, 76
    as social work goal, 17-18
Encuento de Lesbianas de Latino
    America y El Caribe, 88-89
Encuentro, 88
Enmeshment, in lesbian
    relationships, 13,71
Equal employment opportunities, 74
Ethnicity, relationship to feminism,
    80
European-American lesbians, 80
European-American society, lesbians
    of color relationship with,
    79-80

Family
    in Asian culture, 78
    coming out to, 90-91
        by adopted lesbians, 51,52,54
        by Latina lesbians, 90-91
    counseling services for, 71
    of Puerto-Rican lesbians, 25
    rejection by, 78
Feminism, relationship to ethnicity, 80

Hartford, Connecticut, Latina lesbian
    community in, 88
Heterosexism
    definition of, 9

internalized, 8
as political force, 9
relationship to dominance, 9-10
relationship to patriarchal
    oppression, 5
relationship to subordination,
    9-10
Hidalgo, Hilda, xiii,xv,xvi-xvii
Hispanic children, cross-cultural
    adoption of, 46
Homophobia
    of European-American society,
        79-80
    institutionalized, 1
    internalized, 8
        relationship to coming out, 49
    of legal system, 72-73,74
    of military, 24,73
    of Native American community,
        77
    relationship to coming out,
        44-45, 48-49
    social, 1
    towards lesbians of color, 72
Homosexual identity development,
    48
Homosexuality, as pathology, 1
Homosexuals
    African-American, 79
    of color, 75-76
    coming out by, 48-49
    Native-American, 79
Houston, Texas, Latina lesbian
    community in, 88
Human immune deficiency (HIV)
    infection, in Latina
    lesbians, 92
Human service organizations
    anti-homophobic activities of, 2
    heterosexist environment of, 4
        case example, 25-39
    lesbian standpoint view of, 38-39
    patriarchy of, 25,31

Identity, definition of, 44
Identity development. *See also* Lesbian
    identity development
    by adopted people, 47-48
    female differentiated from male, 44
Interviews, with lesbians of color, 15
"Invisibility," of lesbians of color,
    24,25,75-76
Irish-Americans, homophobia of, 89

*Journal of Gay & Lesbian Social
    Services*, 2
Journals, homosexual and lesbian, 2

Klepfisz, Irena, 65
Korean-American lesbian, personal
    narrative by, 61-66

Las Buenas Amigas, 88,89
Latina lesbians, 85-100
    coming out by, 86,90-91
    developmental case history of,
        86-91
Latin Americans, homophobia of, 89
Latinos, "passing" by, 24
Legal system, homophobia of,
    72-73,74
Lesbian and Gay People of Color
    Steering Committee, 89
Lesbian and Gay Pride March, New
    York City, 89
Lesbian community, adopted lesbians'
    attitudes towards, 56
Lesbian identity, as cultural identity, 48
Lesbian identity development
    by adopted lesbians, issues in
        adoptive and sexual identity,
            54-55
        adoptive parents/family, 51
        attitudes towards adoption,
            51,52-53
        attitudes towards lesbian
            community, 56

birth parents/family, 54
relationships, 50-51,59
search for birth parents, 52,
    53,58
support group membership,
    45,56-57
therapy/counseling
    experiences, 51
empowerment and, 76
by lesbians of color, 70-71, 76-78
model of, 44-45
mothers' role in, 44,45
obstacles to, 48
as political response, 45
positive, 48
Lesbianism
as cognitive posture, 9,13,16
definition of, 9
as pathology, 9
Lesbians
"closeted," 49
cognitive, 9,13,16
European-American, 80
Lesbians of color
coming out by, 71
multicultural context of, 8
relationship with
    European-American
    society, 79-80
social service needs of, 67-83
    conflict with Caucasian
        society issue, 79-80
    conflict with community of
        origin issue, 78-79
    cultural and social change
        needs, 73-74
    identity issues, 76-78
    identity needs, 70-71
    lesbian identity issue, 75-76
    loss/threatened loss needs,
        72-73
    material needs, 70
    relationship needs, 71
    social workers' perception of,
        68-81

Life story, as methodological
    framework, 27-30
Los Angeles, Latina lesbian
    community in, 88
Loss, experienced by lesbians of
    color, 71-72
"Loving perception," 12-14,15

Male community, lesbianism as
    threat to, 9,78
Marginality, of Latino lesbians,
    86,90
Marriage, lesbian/homosexual, 74
Master of Social Work programs, gay
    and lesbian curriculum, 30
Medicine men, homosexual, 79
Mennis, Bernice, 65
Mental health, definition of, 37
Mestiza consciousness, 15-16
Mestizo characteristics, 24
Mexican culture, patriarchy of, 78
Miami, Florida, Latina lesbian
    community in, 88
Military, homophobic discrimination
    in, 24,73
Mother, role in lesbian identity
    development, 44,55

Narratives, by lesbians of color, 15
National Association of Social
    Workers, 1,30,33-34
Native-American children
    boarding schools for, 79
    cross-cultural adoption of, 46
Native-American community
    acceptance of gays and lesbians
        by, 79
    homophobia of, 77
    oppression of, 8
Native-American lesbians, 77
Networks, of Latina lesbians,
    88,89,92
New Jersey, anti-homophobic
    discrimination laws in, 73

New York City, Latina lesbian
community in, 86,88,89
Norms, internalized, 38

Oppression
coming out as response to, 45
compartmentalization of, 90
by dominant culture, 8-9
heterosexist, 10
"invisibility" as response to,
24,25,75-76
of lesbians, 9,75
of lesbians of color, 4,72
prioritization of, 68,90
Oppressors, privileges of, 10-11
Oral histories, of lesbians of color, 15

Parker, Pat, 7-8
"Passing," 24
in the workplace, case example
of, 31-37
Patriarchy
of human services organizations,
27,31
of Mexican culture, 78
oppression of women by, 5
People of color. *See also* African
Americans;
African-American children;
African-American
community; Asian-American
lesbians; Latina lesbians;
Lesbians of color;
Native-American children;
Native-American
community;
Native-American lesbians;
Puerto-Rican culture;
Puerto-Rican lesbians
collective versus individual
experiences of, 11
Perceptions, arrogant, 12

Preferred sameness model, of
discrimination, 3
Privilege(s)
heterosexual, 38-39
of oppressors, 10-11
Professional literature, lesbians of
color issues in, 2,75
Public/private dichotomy,
xv,5,10,24-27
case example of, 26-27,28-39
Puerto-Rican culture
codes of sexual behavior in, 79
socialization in, 26
Puerto-Rican lesbians
coming out by, 91
employment discrimination
towards, 25
families of, 25
as human service organization
employees, case example
of, 25-39
Puerto Rican Parade, New York City,
87,89

Racism
of human service organizations, 4
institutional, 4,72
internalized, 8,24
relationship to sexism,
heterosexism and classism,
10
towards Korean-American
lesbians, 62-63
towards Native-American
lesbians, 77
Reality, of lesbians of color,
12-14,15
Relationship needs, of lesbians of
color, 71
Relationships, enmeshment in, 13,71
Rutgers University Library, 2

St. Patrick's Day Parade, New York
City, 89

San Francisco, Latina lesbian
    community in, 88
Separation, in male identity
    development, 44
Sexism
    coming out as response to, 45
    of human service organizations, 4
    internalized, 8
Show de Christina, El, 87
Smith College School for Social
    Work, 65
Social change programs, 73-74
Socialization, in Puerto-Rican
    society, 26
Social service needs, of lesbians of
    color, 67-83
    conflict with Caucasian society
        issue, 79-80
    conflict with community of
        origin issue, 78-79
    cultural and social change needs,
        73-74
    identity issues, 76-78
    identity needs, 70-71
    lesbian invisibility issue, 75-76
    loss/threatened loss needs, 71-73
    material needs, 70
    relationship needs, 71
Social work, empowerment-related
    goals of, 17-18
Social workers, multicultural
    competence of, 7-21
    awareness development for, 8-12
    knowledge development for, 8,
        12-16
    self-examination for, 12
    skill development for, 8,16-18
Spiritual needs, of lesbians of color, 73
Standpoint theory, 3,5,26
    lesbian, applied to human service
        organizations, 38-39
    "loving perception" concept of,
        12-14,15
Subordinate groups, oppression of, 3

Subordination, relationship to
    heterosexism, 9-10
Support groups
    for adolescent lesbians, 71
    for adopted lesbians, 45,56-57
    for Latina lesbians, 87,92
    for lesbians of color, 71,72

Texas, Latina lesbian community in,
    88
Trouble, 18
"Two-spirited people," in Native-
    American culture, 79

Victimism, 37

Women, subordination to men, 8
Work environment, heterosexism of,
    23-24
    case example of, 25-39

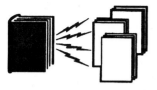

Haworth
DOCUMENT DELIVERY
SERVICE

This valuable service provides a single-article order form for any article from a Haworth journal.

- *Time Saving:* No running around from library to library to find a specific article.
- *Cost Effective:* All costs are kept down to a minimum.
- *Fast Delivery:* Choose from several options, including same-day FAX.
- *No Copyright Hassles:* You will be supplied by the original publisher.
- *Easy Payment:* Choose from several easy payment methods.

Open Accounts Welcome for ...
- Library Interlibrary Loan Departments
- Library Network/Consortia Wishing to Provide Single-Article Services
- Indexing/Abstracting Services with Single Article Provision Services
- Document Provision Brokers and Freelance Information Service Providers

---

MAIL or *FAX* THIS ENTIRE ORDER FORM TO:

Haworth Document Delivery Service
The Haworth Press, Inc.
10 Alice Street
Binghamton, NY 13904-1580

or FAX: 1-800-895-0582
or CALL: 1-800-342-9678
9am-5pm EST

PLEASE SEND ME PHOTOCOPIES OF THE FOLLOWING SINGLE ARTICLES:

1) Journal Title: _____

   Vol/Issue/Year: _____ Starting & Ending Pages: _____

   Article Title: _____

2) Journal Title: _____

   Vol/Issue/Year: _____ Starting & Ending Pages: _____

   Article Title: _____

3) Journal Title: _____

   Vol/Issue/Year: _____ Starting & Ending Pages: _____

   Article Title: _____

4) Journal Title: _____

   Vol/Issue/Year: _____ Starting & Ending Pages: _____

   Article Title: _____

(See other side for Costs and Payment Information)

COSTS: Please figure your cost to order quality copies of an article.

1. Set-up charge per article: $8.00

    ($8.00 × number of separate articles) _____

2. Photocopying charge for each article:

    1-10 pages: $1.00 _____

    11-19 pages: $3.00 _____

    20-29 pages: $5.00 _____

    30+ pages: $2.00/10 pages _____

3. Flexicover (optional): $2.00/article _____

4. Postage & Handling: US: $1.00 for the first article/

    $.50 each additional article _____

    Federal Express: $25.00 _____

    Outside US: $2.00 for first article/

    $.50 each additional article _____

5. Same-day FAX service: $.35 per page _____

GRAND TOTAL: _____

METHOD OF PAYMENT: (please check one)

❑ Check enclosed   ❑ Please ship and bill. PO # _____

    (sorry we can ship and bill to bookstores only! All others must pre-pay)

❑ Charge to my credit card: ❑ Visa; ❑ MasterCard; ❑ Discover;

    ❑ American Express;

Account Number: _____ Expiration date: _____

Signature: ✗ _____

Name: _____ Institution: _____

Address: _____

_____

City: _____ State: _____ Zip: _____

Phone Number: _____ FAX Number: _____

MAIL or *FAX* THIS ENTIRE ORDER FORM TO:

Haworth Document Delivery Service	**or FAX:** 1-800-895-0582
The Haworth Press, Inc.	**or CALL:** 1-800-342-9678
10 Alice Street	9am-5pm EST)
Binghamton, NY 13904-1580	